Managerial Decentralization

Managerial Decentralization

A Study of the General
Electric Philosophy

Ronald G. Greenwood
University of Wisconsin—LaCrosse

Lexington Books
D.C. Heath and Company
Lexington, Massachusetts
Toronto   London

Library of Congress Cataloging in Publication Data

Greenwood, Ronald G.
   Managerial decentralization; a study of the General Electric philosophy.

   Includes bibliographical references.
   1. General Electric Company. 2. Decentralization in management—Case studies. I. Title.
HD9695.U54G4378   658.4'02   73-18416
ISBN 0-669-91793-1

Published simultaneously in Canada.

Printed in the United States of America.

International Standard Book Number: 0-669-91793-1

Library of Congress Catalog Card Number: 73-18416

Contents

List of Figures

Foreword

Most large companies and many of the smaller ones have been resorting to decentralization for several decades. This organizational preference represents the effort to reduce the burden on the chief executive and partly an attempt to accelerate growth. The composite pattern is a delegation of authority and responsibility for given decision-making to as low a level in the management hierarchy that can support it. By proper support is meant the availability of the information needed, the capability of personnel, and, importantly, their willingness to make the decisions required.

The main advantage of decentralization is that decisions are made closer to the scene of action. The department manager, for example, with all the necessary information before him can make decisions focused on needs and resources as he sees them. Before decentralization, decisions of this kind had to be made at the home office, perhaps on the basis of pins on a chart or statistics in a not too recent report.

Decentralization as an organization pattern has deep tap roots although this movement did not become really widespread until after World War II and particularly during the 1950s. Historically, the movement probably began with Henry V. Poor's proposals for the reorganization of the American railroads in the 1850s. These early stirrings of decentralization sought a "science of management" that would offset diminishing returns in a prototype of large scale organization. Poor's suggestions were applied by Daniel McCallum, general superintendent on the Erie Railroad beginning in 1854, and were later used with much success in organizing the railroad transport system during the Civil War.

The first successful large-scale plan of decentralization in manufacturing industry was probably that presented in 1920 to W.C. Durant, president of General Motors, by Alfred P. Sloan, Jr., then G.M. vice president. General Motors at that time had much interlocking management with Du Pont. This remarkable document largely formed the basis of the present General Motors and Du Pont organizations and was later used as a pattern by many other companies.

This theory of decentralization was based on a concept somewhat akin to the theory of atomistic competition. That is, each self-sufficient activity of the corporation would operate on its own within the overall framework of the rules of a free-enterprise system. Freedom of operation would make it possible for each activity and its leadership to contribute to the maximum of their abilities in the light of their superior knowledge of the local situation. Freedom of operation was tempered by veto power, but a coordinated control system set the framework within which the veto would be exercised, and this system provided for accountability.

This ideology was put in the form of statements, speeches, and letters and was frequently repeated and reinforced by example. Undoubtedly, "decentralized operations and coordinated controls" had a powerful appeal to able men. It was inspirational because it gave promise of greater opportunity for the individual. It was intellectually convincing because it pointed out a way of overcoming the problem of diminishing returns from management as size increased. It kept within bounds that individualistic and separatist group of management that was the essence of decentralization in practice.

A later program of decentralization was developed and carried out at the Westinghouse Electric Corporation by A.W. Robertson, Ralph Kelly, and F.D. Newbury during the years 1936 to 1939; it proved to be extremely successful. Standard Oil of California was another pioneer in systematic organization planning under L.L. Purkey. Other outstanding examples of decentralization include programs at Continental Oil and the Ford Motor Company.

One of the most exciting and dynamic decentralizations of all took place in General Electric in the 1950s. In the pages that follow, Ronald Greenwood brings into sharp focus the thinking, the concepts, and the rationale that brought it about. It is a truly definitive study not only of the changes that took place in General Electric but of the principles and observations of decentralization in action.

Ernest Dale

Preface

Writing is a form of working out one's confusion. To that aim these eight chapters are dedicated. The challenge has been to offer a better understanding of decentralization as developed by one of the most famous of the decentralized firms—the General Electric Company. To aid in the understanding of such a complicated structure as this extremely large and diversified company, it is necessary to simplify the subject for research purposes and then to convey an analysis which, if factual, will retain the complex substance of the study.

In Chapter 1 the word *decentralization* is defined. The term is elusive, having a multitude of meanings. In a strict definition, as Dale and Koontz point out, all organizations are decentralized.[1] Decentralization represents organizational structures with a variety of patterns. The succeeding chapters define "decentralization" as it is found in only one organization—General Electric. The purpose is to discuss what decentralization has been and is at General Electric, not to make any claims that their decentralization is the best, the most traditional, or the most progressive. General Electric was chosen because its style of decentralization is so often used as a model for other organizations, yet very little has been published on the subject.

One of the goals of this book is to show that the reorganization and decentralization structure developed at General Electric, especially from 1950 to 1970, is based on a great deal of thought, and that it is built upon a well-conceived philosophical foundation. The decentralization structure within the company was not an accident, it was developed through the course of hundreds of man years of planning. On the other hand, I will not attempt either to prove or to disprove that General Electric developed the best in-depth managerial and organizational philosophy found in American business, a belief held by many academicians and practitioners.

I will try to show that General Electric was well organized, in both an academic and a practical sense. That is, it developed a plan for decentralization that was perhaps as detailed as any plan for corporate reorganization and, because of its place in time, it is more comprehensive than the Sloan plan for General Motors developed three decades before.[2] No attempt will be made to claim that the organization structure at General Electric made the company the success it is. The company certainly is larger than it was before decentralization, but the dynamics of the environment prevent any realistic laboratory study to show the effects of organization change upon size. Certainly, the structure affected the financial, physical, and emotional situation of the company, but one cannot determine whether the overall effect was positive or negative. Theodore Quinn (retired Vice President, General Electric Company) believed that with the enormous capital and market power the company possesses, General Electric could be the most poorly managed company in the country and still be a high financial success, so great is its base.[3]

No attempt will be made to examine the validity of the particular type of decentralization which General Electric chose, as opposed to other possible types of structure. Such a concern is highly academic and would require examination of alternative decentralization structures. That topic is held for other investigations of the company. A return to centralization would be unthinkable, from the standpoint of size and complexity within the firm. The company cannot go back twenty years. It is almost a completely different organization, mentally and physically.

Chapter 2 presents a short history of the General Electric Company. For the most part, the company's growth has been a logical and organic process. Since 1892, General Electric has been basically in the business of generation, distribution, and application of electric power. Drucker says that today the firm is the most conglomerate of all companies, yet it is still within the basic scope of the electric power industry.[4] In 1950, GE was a highly centralized conglomerate company; by 1960, it was highly decentralized. The 1950s were extremely turbulent for the company because of the organizational changes, yet the firm doubled in size, growing from a $2.2 billion firm in 1950 to a $4.4 billion firm in 1960. The 1960s again saw the company double, growing to $8.8 billion in sales in 1970.[5] Today, 1973, it is above the $10-billion-dollar level.

Alfred Chandler, who has done extensive work in studying the history and the organization structures of American big business, explains that General Electric, before 1939, was basically a functional organization with some autonomous divisions, such as X-Ray, Carboloy, and so forth, attached to the structure. The Home Appliance area, being a profitable business, had a merchandise department distinct from the sales department of the company. The latter was used by the nonappliance departments of the firm. At first, the company developed home appliances only to increase the demand for electricity, and hence to increase the demand for the company's major products for the generation and conducting of electricity. Even though home appliances had a marketing organization, all designing, manufacturing, and assembling were supervised by the older functional departments. Thus, it can be said formally that the firm was highly centralized. Chandler says, "Until 1939, however, General Electric executives did little to relate the work of the Merchandise Department and the other more autonomous new product divisions with the older functional departments or the company's central office."[6]

The major organizational changes did not begin until after the first retirement of Swope and Young in 1940. Charles Wilson began to reshape the company but World War II delayed his plans. In a recent letter, Wilson commented, "My own design and desire, as early as 1930, was decentralization, but by the time I became President in 1940 we were on the verge of a world war."[7] Such a statement is not idle boasting–in 1929, at the company's Association Island executive meeting, Wilson made a speech listing the advantages of and the need for decentralization. He advocated "a more complete decentralization of those departments which are now partly decentralized ... [and] the adoption of vertical or decentralized type to the extent that it is practicable by other departments."[8]

The central point of this book is the great reorganization of 1951 and its consequences as developed by Ralph Cordiner. Chandler says, "Cordiner's reorganization went further than those in any other company studied here [a list including most of the largest companies in America], both in the erection of a large number of relatively small administrative units, and in the methods developed to administer these units."[9]

Most of this book concentrates on the theory, knowledge, concepts, and planning at General Electric. Only Chapters 4, 5, and 6 make any real attempt to go beyond this to discuss the actual practice of management—the experience and expediency—which help to make the real world somewhat different from the philosophy developed at GE.

Sincere acknowledgment is made to the faculty of the College of Business Administration at the University of Oklahoma, and especially to Dr. Ronald B. Shuman, whose guidance cannot be overstated, and to Dr. William H. Keown, for his critical comments.

Appreciation is expressed for the help received from the General Electric Company and its employees, both past and present, and especially Harold F. Smiddy, who spent many hours with this author; Philip D. Reed; Lemuel Boulware; Jack S. Parker; Paul Mills; and Hugh Estes, each of whom contributed much in the way of helpful suggestions. This appreciation of thanks should not be interpreted as implying that the company is necessarily in agreement with the contents of the book, or that this is an authorized publication. Such is not the case. The company was kind enough to allow me to interview numerous employees and to use company documents for investigation, and has allowed me to publish a multitude of quotes. Various members of General Electric have read the manuscript and have offered suggestions, but at no time did they request I include or exclude any material.

Dr. Peter F. Drucker assisted in no small manner, not only with his usual insight, but also with his encouragement to push on. Most of the manuscript was typed by Mrs. William J. Greenwood, June C. Starck, and Patsy Stephens.

Finally, this author is indebted to William J. Greenwood, past General Electric employee and currently Vice President of Chase Manhattan Bank, N.A., who gave lavishly of his time, advice, criticism, and suggestions, without which this work could never have been completed.

The opinions and any errors are strictly the author's.

1 Decentralization

Defining decentralization is no easy task. Every company that claims to be decentralized defines it differently. General Electric, Westinghouse, General Motors, DuPont, and Standard Oil of New Jersey, perhaps the best-known firms connected with a decentralized managerial philosophy, constitute only a few of the decentralized companies. Alfred D. Chandler, Jr., whose outstanding and in-depth article, "Managerial Decentralization: A Historical Analysis," published in 1956, claims that almost all of the fifty largest firms in the nation (size based on 1948 assets) were decentralized.[1] He goes on to write about the few centralized giant firms as follows: "In 1955 a number of the most highly centralized organizations among the top fifty industrial firms were those still dominated by men well beyond the normal compulsory retirement age."[2] Chandler studies decentralization by looking at ten different industries (chemical, electrical, automotive, steel, food, and so forth). He studies decentralization by tracing its history, starting with DuPont's concentration on decentralization near the turn of the century, and how DuPont influenced General Motor's organizational arrangement in the 1920s.[3] Yet Chandler does not define what he means by decentralization. In order to establish a definition of decentralization, the leading writers in the field should be consulted. They include Donaldson Brown[4] of DuPont and General Motors; Ralph Cordiner[5] of General Electric; Ernest Dale,[6] Consultant and Educator; John Dearden,[7] Educator concentrating on the financial control side of decentralization, and Alfred P. Sloan, Jr.,[8] also of General Motors. From these and various other contributors, we will try to develop one usable definition for "decentralization" in terms of big business.

"Decentralization" is not a precise or absolute term. Any attempt to make it an absolute term definitely would negate its value as a descriptive device. If the term is defined strictly in terms of General Electric philosophy, then it will not necessarily describe General Motors or Westinghouse. Yet more precision in definition should be offered than is currently found in the hodgepodge offered in the literature. The term does mean different things to different people. Starting from a pure definition and working towards a usable one, we can begin by noting that decentralization has at least two common meanings. One is geographic decentralization, which refers to the location of factories, offices, the spreading out of the companies' physical plant facilities. The other generally held meaning is decentralization of authority, which refers to the spreading out of the authority, responsibility, and decision-making to members of the organization other than the dominant executive. We will exclude geographic

1

decentralization and concentrate on decentralization of decision-making authority; managerial decentralization as opposed to geographic decentralization.[9] Ernest Dale claims, "The term decentralization itself means the delegation of business decisions by the owners to their immediate representatives [the board of directors and the chief executive], and then to others further down in the management hierarchy."[10] This definition, for practical purposes, is unusable, as all large organizations would be considered decentralized. Even those large business organizations which most managerial experts consider as having centralized management would be considered decentralized under the above definition. Perhaps this definition was used by Alfred D. Chandler, Jr., allowing him to claim that most of America's fifty largest firms are decentralized. In some sense all organizations are decentralized. Koontz and O'Donnell are in full agreement with Dale when they point out:

Decentralization of authority is a fundamental phase of delegation; to the extent that authority is not delegated, it is centralized. Absolute centralization in one person is conceivable, but it implies no subordinate managers and therefore no structured organization. Consequently, it can be said that some decentralization characterizes all organizations. On the other hand, there cannot be absolute decentralization, for if a manager should delegate *all* his authority, his status as a manager would cease; his position would be eliminated; there would, again, be no organization.[11]

Henri Fayol stated in 1916 that "centralization belongs to the natural order,"[12] but he was not using "centralization" in the pure sense, for he continued, "The question of centralization or decentralization is a simple question of proportion, it is a matter of finding the optimum degree for the particular concern."[13] Fayol ends with his definition of decentralization: "Everything which goes to increase the importance of the subordinate's role is decentralization; everything which goes to reduce it is centralization."[14]

Some managers have not read Fayol's definition well, for they have assumed that the number of decisions made at lower levels determines the degree of decentralization. It is not the number of decisions allowed to be made by subordinates, as so many executives incorrectly believe, but the importance of the decisions made at lower levels which matters. Delegating numerous little unimportant decisions and keeping one highly influential decision at the top is not decentralization. Ernest Dale conducted a limited survey for the American Management Association and found that delegation of decision-making was more widespread in 1952 than in 1942, and that decentralization was believed to be widespread in 1952.[15] But he was able to comment:

Despite all the talk we hear about decentralization and the delegation of decision making, an examination of the actual activities of chief executives discloses that they continue to make most or all major decisions, either directly or through a formal framework of strict rules, checks and balances, informal instructions, and through mental compulsion on the part of subordinates to act as the boss would act. Chief executives also make final decisions on matters which are relatively or absolutely unimportant.[16]

Decentralization is not only the delegation of the unimportant decisions to the lowest possible level, upholding the principle of management by exception, but it means delegation of many major decisions to lower levels, again upholding the principle of management by exception. (The principle of management by exception is the belief that all decisions should be made at the lowest possible level and that only decisions can be moved up a level if the lowest level did not have the ability (authority, knowledge, and so forth) to make the decisions. It ultimately means that decisions made by the president could not have been made at a lower level.)

The difference between what is advocated and what is practiced may vary widely, as Dale, Henry Albers,[17] Helen Baker and Robert R. France,[18] and Mayer N. Zald,[19] among others, have found.

Peter F. Drucker, in his landmark book *The Practice of Management*, spurns the use of centralization altogether, in agreement with Dale's belief that all large organizations are decentralized. Drucker used the terms "federal decentralization"—the organizing of activities into autonomous product businesses each having its own market and product and own profit-and-loss center—as the common meaning of decentralization. The other term he uses is "functional decentralization," which is the setting up of integrated units handling a major and distinct stage of the business.[20] This last term is not the same as the traditional organization by functions—marketing, production, finance, and so forth—or by related skills. "Functional decentralization" is organization by stage of process. Drucker says, "Some of the large companies are today engaged in thinking through engineering organization and in putting the engineering jobs where they belong according to the logic of the work to be done rather than according to the tools needed."[21]

The weaknesses found for "functional decentralization" are the same as weaknesses found for any functional organization. Every functional manager tends to know his area well, but not other areas. Each functional manager considers his area the most important, tries to build it up and may subordinate the welfare of other functions. Functionalism makes men specialists, and therefore a narrowing of vision may occur, making the specialist unfit for general management.

Both "federal decentralization" and "functional decentralization" are found in most businesses. Drucker points out that they are not competitive but can be complementary.[22] Yet, because of the weaknesses in the use of solely functional organizational structure, the trend today is for the larger company to decentralize federally—organization by autonomous product lines. Of the two, federal and functional decentralization, federal is the more effective and more productive, according to Drucker.[23] Small firms do not need "federal decentralization," for they are an autonomous product business. The organizational problem for big firms was clearly defined by Donaldson Brown when, in 1927, he wrote: "That problem is to combine the economical advantages of modern business, with as little sacrifice as possible of that intimate control and development of managerial ability that is the character of the well managed small business."[24]

Since World War II managerial decentralization (or federal decentralization, for those who prefer Drucker's terminology) has been adopted or developed by Ford and Chrysler, General Electric and Westinghouse, all the major chemical companies, most of the oil companies, the largest insurance companies, and many of the larger banks (General Motors had it by 1923 and DuPont developed it by 1920).[25]

What is this managerial decentralization? Basically, it is the method of combining the advantages of large-scale operation with the advantages of a well-managed small business. It is the development of a number of independent profit-and-loss centers within a larger organization. The profit-and-loss center allows top management to measure the ability of the managers of each section or division. It allows top management to control each section. Profit-and-loss centers allow each manager in the center to measure himself. The major decision which affects the profit and loss must be made by the manager who is being measured by the profit or loss. In other words, if profit and loss is one aspect of measuring a manager's value, then he must have the power to make as many decisions as possible which affect his grade. Thus, decentralization must push down not only minor decisions, but major decisions as well; all decisions which affect the evaluation of a manager must be made by the manager being measured.

Although decentralization differs from firm to firm, three organizational principles have emerged for most of the decentralized organizations. They are, as Alfred D. Chandler, Jr., found:

1. A number of autonomous operating units whose managers handle the day-to-day operating decisions are responsible for the financial performance of their unit, and have the line authority and staff assistance commensurate with this responsibility.
2. The organization has built up a central advisory staff of specialists which provide services to the operating divisions and help top executives carry out their functions, particularly that of coordinating the activities of the division.
3. The organization includes a top management group which not only coordinates but also supervises the divisions (by reviewing and analyzing divisional operating and financial performances and by taking executive action on the basis of these analyses).[26]

Decentralization relates to the authority to make decisions. Decentralization is a process, as Bernard Baum in his dissertation on *Decentralization in a*

Bureaucracy notes, and "delegation is the technique for implementing this process."[27] Therefore, a major principle of decentralization, as widely stated, is "Authority to take or initiate action should be delegated as close to the scene of action as possible."

Delegation is defined by Harold Stieglitz as "the act of entrusting to someone else [a subordinate] part of the job the person [superior] is expected to carry out."[28] Equally adequate definition is offered by Mooney and Riley: "Delegation means the conferring of a specified authority by a higher authority."[29]

Decentralization relates to how authority is delegated rather than to the grouping of activities. Decisions are delegated to the lowest level where authority, competency, and prestige can be found, to the level and manager who is responsible for the actual performance. This is what R.C. Davis terms the "Principle of Decentralized Decisions."[30] This must be done, as Stieglitz puts it, "without relaxing necessary control over the policy or the standardization of procedure."[31]

In discussing the nature of decentralization Dale stated that the degree of decentralization of authority in a company is increased by:

1. The greater the number of decisions made lower down the management hierarchy.
2. The more important the decisions made lower down the management hierarchy. For example, the greater the sum of capital expenditure that can be approved by the plant manager without consulting anyone else, the greater the degree of decentralization in this field.
3. The more functions affected by decisions made at lower levels. Thus, companies which permit only operational decisions to be made at separate branch plants are less decentralized than those which also permit financial and personnel decisions at branch plants.
4. The less checking required on the decisions. Decentralization is greatest when no check at all must be made; less when superiors have to be informed of the decision after it has been made; still less if superiors have to be consulted before the decision is made. The fewer people to be consulted, and the lower they are on the management hierarchy, the greater the degree of decentralization.[32]

Decentralization is not usefully applicable to all organizations, nor will it in itself insure good management. The extent to which authority can be delegated, the extent to which profit centers can be organized, the extent to which operations can be coordinated, are determined by a number of factors—the most important of which is size. The larger an organization, the more the likelihood that decentralization is needed and will be found. There is a direct relationship between the size of an organization, in terms of numbers of people, and the numbers of decisions which must be made. Largeness of size and centralization of structure will raise the cost and lower the effectiveness of decisions. Decisions in centralized organizations are pushed toward the top where they accumulate, which means higher-cost personnel will work on them and the decision will be made farther away from the point of the problem. Ernest Dale notes that "The cost of making decisions generally tends to be higher the farther away they are made from the point at which the problem arises. . . . The decision itself may be less satisfactory."[33] Dale,[34] Sisk,[35] and Koontz and O'Donnell[36] all note that with largeness is found complexity, which may result in overburdening top management and multiply the difficulties in the communications process.

The difficulties caused by size can be somewhat overcome by breaking the whole into sections that are of a manageable size. Exact optimum size cannot be arbitrarily stated. Some observers believe it to be 1000 persons, others 2500 or more; some claim 100 or so as being the best economic size for decentralized units.[37]

A second factor in determining how much decentralization is desirable is the philosophy of management, especially top management. It is a matter not only of their philosophy, but of their real actions. As George A. Smith, Jr., points out, "Many executives pay at least lip service to the ideal of a 'democratic' organization [decentralization]; fewer are willing to foot the bill that they fear may be involved if they give subordinates more authority."[38] Decentralization must be a way of life. It has been said that "decentralization is 95 percent an attitude of mind."[39] Decentralization cannot be a reality, no matter what the organization charts and manuals claim, unless top and even middle management truly believe and practice delegation.

Management philosophy is closely tied with management personalities. The organizational arrangement is modified by personalities found in each particular organization. (Defining personality as the sum total of the skills, abilities, interests, and personal characteristics.) As Lieutenant Colonel Urwick has put it so well, the problem is one of personality—in part it is *personal*, in part it is *personnel.*[40] If any of the top management feels insecure and cannot delegate, then decentralization stops at the top, no matter what is considered corporate policy. On the other hand, willingness to delegate by the top may run into difficulties through unwillingness from the middle managers to accept delegation and responsibility. The personalities of most of the managers and all of the key managers must be such that decentralization is not only a theory but a reality. It means that the supervisor must have confidence in the competence of the subordinate receiving the delegation and the subordinate must actually have the competence to make the proper decisions with his delegated authority.[41]

A major factor in determining the degree of decentralization is cost. There are at least two types of cost affected by decentralization. (The possible increased costs of communications is not to be overlooked, as it too creates cost. This will be discussed in Chapter 3.) One is the added cost, in dollars and cents, caused by the added number of management personnel and the duplication of jobs found in decentralized organizations. The other type of cost may be intangible, such as a company's reputation, its competitive position, and morale of employees, which may be upset by a mistake made by a lower-level employee's decision. The reputation effects on a firm can be seen by what happened to General Electric's and Westinghouse's total company image in the early 1960s just by the price-fixing practices of a few of its divisions out of the well over one hundred divisions which make up these two giant corporations. Delegation of decisions, therefore, is limited by the ability of subordinates to make them, and by the image which incorrect decisions will inflict upon the organization. This is why decisions involving hundreds of thousands of dollars can be delegated to such surprisingly low levels in many firms, and why other companies allow only decisions involving less than five hundred dollars to be made at the same level.

A similar problem, and often part of the cost factor, is the need for uniformity of policy for the organization. Uniform policies have many advantages, such as standardized accounting, statistics, and financial records, which make it easier to compare departments, file for taxes, deal with unions, and staff personnel to "suggest" policy. Yet many firms go to great lengths to make sure that some policies will not be completely uniform. Koontz and O'Donnell believe:

When a company decentralizes authority to encourage individual initiative, certain business policies may be as varied as the individual managers make them. Many companies encourage this variety in all except major matters hoping that out of such nonuniformity may come managerial innovation, progress, competition between organizational units, improved morale and efficiency, and a supply of promotable managerial manpower.[42]

Information is a key to decision-making. The person making a decision requires adequate information pertaining to that decision. Therefore, delegation of decision-making cannot be pushed below the level at which all information pertinent to the decision is available.

The degree of the dynamics of the business situation has great impact on the amount of decentralization. Old and well-established or status businesses have a tendency to centralize or recentralize. In these situations uniformity in policy is desired, as fewer major decisions are made than are found in the more dynamic situations.[43] In contrast, Dale has found that when a firm hits hard times competition may well foster centralization, as top management feels that the organization cannot afford mistakes and greatly centralizes the decision-making process.[44]

Mayer N. Zald mentions two other points affecting the degree of decentralization. One is that the more disparate the production lines and technologies of the organization, the greater probability of granting more autonomy to the divisions. He also notes that the greater the profitability of a division, in terms of the other divisions, the more independence it will be given. It would then follow that if a major division suffers a reversal, the crackdown of top management would be more likely than would be found in the lesser satellite.[45]

Peter F. Drucker, with his astute perception, has discovered five basic rules which are essential for the structure of a successful decentralized organization. His first rule is that both the parts and the center must be strong. Some people may believe that decentralization means weakening the center by strengthening the decentralized units, but such a belief is a mistake. As Drucker points out, "Federal [managerial] decentralization requires strong guidance from the center through the setting of clear, meaningful, and high objectives for the whole."[46] The center, therefore, must demand a high degree of business performance and control by measurements. Control by measurements shall be discussed shortly.

The second rule is that each autonomous unit must be large enough to support the needed management, and at the same time "small enough" for that team to "get its arms around" and do an effective job. The third Drucker rule is that each decentralized unit must have potential for growth. Fourth, the jobs of the managers must present enough scope and challenge to each individual contributor. This point is valid for all jobs in centralized or decentralized firms. In decentralized firms it should be carefully watched to prevent breaking jobs and units down so far that the scope and challenge of the jobs are not large enough to allow the managers and units to grow. Drucker's fifth rule is that each decentralized unit should exist with its own job and its own market and/or product, and where decentralized units come in touch it should be in competition with one another, as in General Motors' Chevrolet and Pontiac divisions. When the units work together—and Drucker says they should never be required to do anything jointly—their relations must be based strictly on business dealings and not on their inability to stand alone.[47]

Trends

The 1950s saw a general trend of the larger American firms to decentralize. In 1962 Theo Haimann was able to say, "a decentralization program has become something of a fad."[48]

The period of the sixties saw more firms decentralize, while at the same time many of the firms that had earlier decentralized turned toward recentralization.

One reason for recentralization appears to be economy. During profit squeezes and recessions companies begin to worry about duplication of effort within the organization. Another stated reason for recent recentralization, as found by Dale, is that decentralization entailed too much loss of control. A third reason offered by firms was changes in circumstances, such as market situations; one firm noted that its recentralization was caused by "changes consonant with changing market and product requirement."[49] Lastly, a few firms attributed recentralization in part to the impact of electronic data-processing equipment (EDP).[50]

Many authors have been predicting for a number of years that EDP will bring about a trend toward recentralization. One article of particular note on this theme is the 1958 *Harvard Business Review* article by Harold J. Leavitt and Thomas L. Whisler entitled "Management in the 1980s." The article presents a strong case for the proposition that the new information technology will reverse the trend toward decentralization and participative management.

One important reason for expecting fast changes in current practices is that information technology will make centralization much easier.

If centralization becomes easier to implement, managers will probably revert to it. Decentralization has, after all, been largely negatively motivated. Top managers have backed into it because they have been unable to keep up with size and technology. They could not design and maintain the huge and complex communication systems that their large, centralized organizations needed. Information technology should make recentralization possible. It may also obviate other major reasons for decentralization. For example, speed and flexibility will be possible despite larger size, and top executives will be less dependent on subordinates because there will be fewer "experience" and "judgment" areas in which the junior men have more working knowledge.[51]

In 1964 Gilbert Burck agreed that computers would reverse the trend toward decentralization.[52] Disagreeing with this premise, Max Ways, in his *Fortune* article of July, 1966, "Tomorrow's Management,"[53] and H. Igor Ansoff, in *Harvard Business Review*,[54] as early as 1965 took issue with the idea of recentralization being caused by the computers. John Dearden, considered by many as one of the top experts in this area, has stated, "I seriously doubt that the increasing use of computers and related information technology will affect top management's ability to control divisional operations, and in particular that it will bring about a trend to recentralization."[55] Dale found in the AMA survey that some companies did mention EDP as one of many reasons for their recentralization, but, he said, "So far it does not appear that EDP has sparked any general trend toward centralization."[56]

Control

Control is another term which needs some discussion. The term is frequently defined, in management, as a three-step process of setting standards, checking performance against the predetermined standards, and correcting any deviations. The word "controls" is not plural for the word "control" in managerial terminology. "Controls" are the methods used to get control. The word "Controls" pertains to means, and "control" to an end. This may be better understood by looking at the achievement of the overall goals of the organization and how subgoals for individual parts are related. Two problems arise: setting the subgoals and seeing that they are achieved. The setting of subgoals is the setting of controls. Information coming from the individual subgoals develops data that are used for two purposes: first, information is developed to make sure that people are following out the subgoals set for them, and second, information is developed to detect whether or not the subgoals are really right to attain the overall organizational goal.

Control, along with planning and organizing, is considered a basic function of management. Most authors take their basic managerial functions from the five offered in 1916 by Henri Fayol, either adding to or subtracting from this basic list. Yet a number of learned authorities do not accept the term "control" as representing a basic managerial function. Luther Gulick in the 1930s, Peter F. Drucker and Earl Brooks in the 1950s, and General Electric, IBM, and Chase Manhattan Bank all agree that the term "control" does not represent a managerial function. Gulick uses the term "budgeting and reporting" to cover the area. Drucker, Brooks, GE, IBM, and Chase all use the term "measuring" to identify the work which the others term "controlling."[5 7]

"Measuring," as used by these authorities, is a concept, or an element, in the manager's work of leading and motivating which encompasses a fundamental method to satisfy every manager's growing needs to obtain, analyze, and understand more and deeper information. This information is also directly available to, and used by, the man whose work is being measured.

Here is the difference from "control." Under the "measuring" philosophy the information is usually not given to some "higher" authority, either to second-guess the man doing the work, or to take the real responsibility of the man's own work upstairs and away from him.

Measuring is a basic industrial, sociological, and managerial working environment concept fitted to the immediate present and the future, and not the past. All people, including managers and nonmanagers at all levels, are more and more seeing themselves as acting with initiative, self-development, self-discipline, and competence as to both their personal work and voluntary teamwork, and as to two-way communication, and needing an opportunity for seeing their individual job whole in its relationship to the work of others in their own area, in their company, and imaginatively and in true perspective, in the whole social, economic, and political world in which they exist.

Measuring effectively relates these natural individual motivation forces to the accomplishment of division and company objectives, as well as to the planning, organizing, and coordinating elements of the manager's work of leading and motivating.

The control process must be built into the organization structure and be part of the responsibility and authority design. Unfortunately, most control systems are designed separately from the organizational design. There is an attempt to "fit" the control process to the organization. "Control and organization have generally been treated independently of each other," says Arnold F. Emich, "thus missing the point of how the organization is to work in practice."[5 8] In designing the organization one has to understand and analyze the actual control of the business, especially with respect to personnel decisions in promotion. "Otherwise," Drucker says, "one designs a system of 'controls' which does not lead to 'control.' One . . . has to think through the actual 'control' system, the personnel decisions, to see whether it really is in agreement with the true needs of the business. Otherwise there is no economic performance."[59]

Centralized Control

To keep a decentralized organization from fragmentation, some central control must develop as a unifying agent. Without some control complete decentralization might permit one division to bankrupt or greatly harm the total firm. Henry Albers aptly puts it, "Organizations cannot survive without coordination and a unity of purpose."[60] Successful decentralization depends upon the development of a system of controls that will permit the extension of the widest practical delegation of authority to the lowest level of management as possible. This is to say, delegation of decision-making should be made to the lowest level without impeding the overall position of the organization. The centralized control allows the top of the organization to hold onto its parts without making all of the decisions. "Unfortunately," Rensis Likert claims, "decentralization usually stops at the plant or divisional level. In companies using decentralization, there is often more centralized control within the decentralized division than existed prior to the occurrence of decentralization."[61] This, of course, might cause a morale problem when the stated philosophy of management is violated.

Management performs two types of control. The first is to set policy, although it is possible for policy to come from outside the organization; i.e., government rules and regulations, or customer specifications. The second type of control, and often a part of the policy-making, is the setting of measurements and standards. Managers have the obligation to determine the modes of measurement, such as return on investment, competitive standing, cost versus output, and so forth. Once the mode of measurement is determined—and more than one mode is normally used—then management must set standards of achievement by which to evaluate effectiveness of division, section, manager, or individual contributor. If management decides on return on investment as the measurement, it might then decide on 15 percent as the standard.

There are a number of types of policy under the general heading of control. The coordination of activities within each operating division and the areas of interdivisional relations is another major area for centralized control. As Donaldson Brown said in 1927, "There must be no undue conflict, competitively, between the product of one division and that of another. There are certain general policies which, if good for one division, are good for all divisions."[62] Then there is policy as a whole, rather than from the viewpoint of one division. Purchases may be more economical if conducted so as to combine the needs of all divisions. Engineering might also be more economical and useful if it reports to the company in general rather than to particular divisions. The organization might decide that advertising as one institution, rather than having each division advertise, is better. General Electric, Westinghouse, DuPont, and General Motors, to a more limited extent, advertise as institutions.

This setting of centralized control through corporate policy does not seem to fit our original definition of control—setting standards, measuring results, and correcting deviations. The reason is that this is a different type of control. Policy-making and measuring are two types of controls. Policy-making, of which setting standards is one type, deals with the future and comes under the managerial planning function. Measuring is a current and continuous function, even to the point of establishing new measurements as it becomes evident that more information is worthwhile. Measuring covers all types of functions of managers, planning, coordinating, and communicating. Measuring decisions come within the broad framework of policy controls. The purpose of policy is to free up the time of managers and to establish common decisions across a broad spectrum. Policy frees the time of managers because they no longer have to search for answers and can spend time on other kinds of planning and decisions. Policy should be determined long before decisions are required for common purposes. Measuring should be determined as a judgment against predetermined standards.

2

A Short History of the General Electric Company

Electrical manufacturing accounts for approximately 8 percent of the total manufacturing activity in the United States and perhaps 3 percent of all economic activity.[1] The use of electricity has doubled every decade since the 1800s and has grown three times as fast as the nation's economy. The industry is dominated by two firms, each having sales in excess of $5 billion in 1972— General Electric ($10,239,500,000)[2] and Westinghouse ($5,086,621,000).[3] At the other end of the spectrum are hundreds of firms specializing in the manufacture of one or two products. The importance of the large firms can be testified to by size alone. In terms of sales, General Electric ranked fourth in the nation for 1972 and Westinghouse fourteenth.[4]

General Electric Under Charles Coffin

Charles Albert Coffin was President of General Electric from its outset in 1892 until 1913, and Chairman of the Board until 1922. General Electric's first organizational structure was centralized into five functional departments (Figure 2-1). This was by design: the formation of General Electric came about by combining two different entities, the Thomson-Houston Electric Company and the Edison General Electric Company. The internal workings of these two firms must have been somewhat decentralized, for in the company's second annual report President Coffin, in January 1894, stated, the "Board had little success in its efforts to centralize and simplify the organization."[5] But Coffin, whose managerial ability should receive much of the credit for General Electric's early success, was able to pull the numerous divisions together into a centralized functional organization. Although General Electric was by far the largest firm in the industry, managerial ability and managerial knowhow were not readily available, nor were the product lines large enough to warrant any other type of organizational setup. At this time the company only had three plants— Schenectady, New York; Lynn, Massachusetts; and Harrison, New Jersey.

Swope to Cordiner

On May 16, 1922, Gerard Swope became the third President of General Electric. He took the reins of office during a depression that was hitting General Electric

13

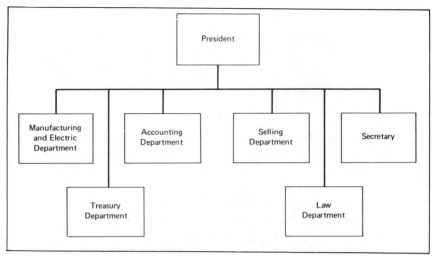

Figure 2-1. General Electric's First Organization Structure—1892

very hard. General Electric had laid off 20,000 men, almost a quarter of its 1920 force. Business had dropped from sales of $318 million in 1920 to $179 million in 1921.[6] The major problem of getting Swope, at the time President of International General Electric,[7] into the presidency of the parent company was how to remove President Rice, who had succeeded Coffin in the post in 1913. Loth notes, "Coffin . . . never had felt that he could leave the reins in Rice's hands."[8] "I never did know how Mr. Coffin persuaded him [Rice] to give up the Presidency," Swope says, "but Rice was used to taking Coffin's orders."[9] Rice was offered an honorary Chairmanship of the Board, created for him, and to everybody's surprise he accepted. Swope and Chairman Owen D. Young then led General Electric from being a major manufacturer into the retailing market, developing the company name into a household word.

The team of Young and Swope led General Electric through the post-World War I reconstruction into the boom of the twenties, through a prostrating depression into a second recovery preceding World War II. Sales passed $415 million in 1929, fell below $137 million in 1933, and rose to nearly $350 million in 1937. Earnings for the same time periods moved from $67,300,000 to $13,400,000 and back to $63,500,000.[10] *Fortune* magazine was able to say in 1940, "During that eighteen years [with Swope and Young] at the head, General Electric had never been in serious trouble. They leave the company with no bonded debt nor any preferred stock outstanding. Their stockholders have never missed a dividend. Their labor has never really struck."[11]

Before World War II, under Gerard Swope, General Electric was not an enormously complex organization. Swope was in complete command with dictatorial powers. *Fortune* termed his attitude and deportment pure Prussian.[12]

The magazine went on to sketch the personality of Swope, in order to analyze the internal management of the firm.

There was never any possible doubt that he [Swope] was running it. Directors' meetings tended to be like a personally conducted tour of certain aspects of General Electric, which Mr. Swope was willing to reveal to the assembled company. He gave no quarter to an advisory committee of high company officers. Below him there were in general two kinds of situations. First, there were committees galore, the subpresidential management resting largely with them rather than with responsible department heads. . . . [Second] a man with an idea that Swope approved could get authority to carry it out, plus a special new title and, probably, an office farther upstairs. . . . Thus, company operations were forever being altered by men suddenly invested with new powers.[13]

There was a definite lack of established management design in the firm. This led some to describe General Electric under Swope as paradoxically successful chaos.[14] By the end of Swope's reign, some in the company became alarmed at the lack of systematic management, and by the uncertainty and indirection of the vast bureaucracy. Organizationally, the firm was not structured to fit the complex needs of the operations. Top management, Swope specifically, gave much of its time to large apparatus, indicating little interest in the fact that it also had a great appliance business. General Electric was founded for the electrical apparatus field and built appliances to stimulate electrical consumption. The role of General Electric was one built on "the benign circle of electric power" philosophy, so well stated by Ralph Cordiner:

A turbine generator installed in a power station makes possible the sale of more lamps, appliances, motors, and other users of power. And as more people buy lamps, appliances and so on, they create the need for another turbine generator and more transmission equipment. Thus, each new use of electricity accelerates the turn of the circle—creating a bigger potential market for General Electric products, not only in end use equipment, but in equipment to produce, transmit, and distribute electric power.[15]

Fortune's description of "paradoxically successful chaos" was best applied to the appliance business, which was "conducted," they claimed, "in a fundamentally haphazard manner."[16] For instance, the refrigerator had parts made in four widely separated plants before being finally assembled. Although General Electric had a good showing in refrigerator sales, the operation was inefficient and costly. In smaller appliances—toasters, clocks, and so forth—General Electric was very inefficient compared with the small independent companies specializing in these products. General Electric was doing about 30 percent of its gross business in appliances, yet it was not managing appliances as a major contributor of the firm.[17]

In 1938, Charles Wilson, Executive Vice President, who was later to succeed

Swope, moved to change this managerially unhealthy situation. He set up a planning committee consisting of one or two key men from each of the firm's main departments, with the objective of giving General Electric a thorough overall review. The committee concluded that in order to progress efficiently the business must adopt two principles: in management, decentralization; and in production, diversification and specialization.[18] The importance of this committee's recommendation is not to be overlooked, for this is the beginning of GE's concerted efforts by top management to decentralize the managerial decision-making to lower ranks. Although the term "decentralization" was perhaps understood much differently in 1938 than in 1951 (or later), this recommendation is the real starting point for the company's decentralization policy, which culminated in Cordiner's reorganization in the 1950s. Wilson became President in 1940, and at once began to reorganize and decentralize, but World War II intervened and he and new Chairman Philip O. Reed went to Washington for the war effort, being replaced by Young as Chairman and Swope as President.

Peace brought Wilson and Reed back to their prewar positions, and also brought Ralph J. Cordiner, who prior to the war was President of the Schick Company, to General Electric as Vice President and Assistant to the President. Under Wilson's leadership, Cordiner gradually developed the organization structure shown in Figure 2-2.

Cordiner, Diversification, and Decentralization

Decentralization had its beginnings in General Electric as early as 1929, when some aspects of it were covered at a company convention of top and middle management held at Association Island on Lake Ontario. The need for the General Electric type of decentralization stems from the complexity of problems inherent in the diversity of the company product lines. When General Electric was first organized, it was principally in heavy apparatus for utilities and light apparatus for street railways and lamps. "Today, it is the most diversified company in the country,"[19] asserts labor expert and ex-General Electric employee Herbert Northrup. It is involved in almost every aspect of the electrical equipment industry, as well as in metallurgy, glass, aerospace, and land-based nuclear power, and is one of the nation's leading chemical manufacturers.

In 1943, Ralph Cordiner was made Assistant to President Gerard Swope (Charles Wilson was still on the War Production Board). His major assignment was to develop a plan for overhauling the management and organization structure of the corporation. After three years of study, he called for a complete reorganization. He said, "Unless we could now put the responsibility and

17

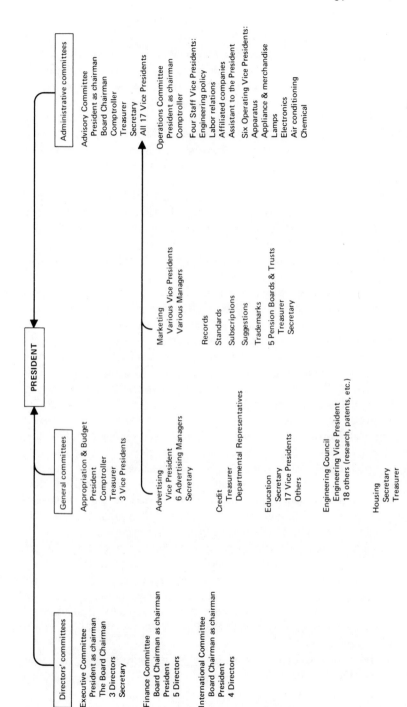

Figure 2-2. Unofficial Organization Chart of General Electric Company (Shortly After World War II). Source: "Mr. Wilson at Work," *Fortune*, vol. 35, no. 5 (May 1947), p. 168.

authority for decision making closer in each case to the scene of the problem, the company would not be able to compete with the hundreds of nimble competitors."[20] At General Electric, "decentralization" meant to keep the strengths afforded by large organizations but adding the flexibility of smaller firms. The key to decentralization is placing responsibility and authority for making business decisions on the level where they are needed. Of course, upper management was retained for long-range planning, guidance, and policy, and to delegate this authority generally to lower echelons. The latter was perhaps the greatest obstacle that Cordiner had to overcome when he first instituted decentralization.

After World War II the company began to implement its bold new program of total decentralization. By 1948 the company had passed the $1.5 billion sales level,[21] and it had detected signs of operational immobility which Cordiner attributed to organizational design weaknesses.

Cordiner became President in December of 1950, and within two years General Electric was reorganized. Cordiner was not due to take over for another two years, but Wilson was called to Washington to team with Sidney Hillman to head up the Korean War Office of Defense Mobilization. Because of Wilson's sudden departure, Cordiner was faced with an immediate problem: should he implement his decentralization policy quickly or slowly?[22] He chose the quick route. Some two thousand top manager jobs were created or redefined; twenty divisions were set up with about seven departments.[23] The functional organization was abolished. The staff or services employees were cut down to a relatively small number of highly experienced men to render assistance and advice. This completely did away with the growing tendency found in American industry of allowing the staff consultants to make the actual decisions by virtue of their position.

The new philosophy and organization meant replacing central control with decentralized control, and the essentially autonomous structuring of about eleven operating product departments. The emphasis was directed to removal of "security, complacency, and mediocrity,"[24] and an installation of an incentive or reward system which was hoped to bring higher and tougher standards.

Under Ralph Cordiner, the decentralization activities followed his well-conceived plan which fit so well with the beliefs of the new generation of company leaders who had grown up during and after the Hawthorne experiments and therefore preached human relations. It brought a new concept of delegated authority, responsibility, and accountability. "Success would bring advancement and reward," noted one-time manager, Dr. Edward Currie. "Failure would be equally swift in its results."[25]

Concern for people is a hallmark of the corporate philosophy of decentralization. In 1945 Vice President Cordiner stated:

In 30 years the areas most seriously demanding management's immediate attention have gone through more than a complete cycle. First, it was the customer and the employee, and these two should have continued first. Then, it was the production backlog itself. Then, it was the customer—in the severest buyer's market of all times. Then, with war, it was production again. Now the equipment and facility problems are largely answered, and the personnel problems rising to an all-time high. In the belief that the personnel problem—or opportunity—is a series of intimate, personal, local cases, we are looking to decentralization to bring top management close to the employee.[26]

In a 1946 paper Cordiner again emphasized the need for organizational discipline and leader skills in terms of human relations:

The problem in all larger companies is to have the members of the organization generally understand that the real test of a good manager is not the multitude of details and the amount of functional operations he performs, but, rather, how well he can visualize the over-all responsibility, assign the work to qualified people, and then see that the employee who is given the assignment, his associates, and the entire organization understands the organization structure and adhere to it.

Our joint objective should be the continual study to simplify, streamline, and strengthen our organization, which means our *human relations and their interdependence* [emphasis added].[27]

Edward M. Currie, Associate Professor of Accounting at the University of Hawaii, worked for General Electric through most of Cordiner's presidency, and for some of that time as Financial Analyst assigned to the President's Office. He tells us that the opportunities for college graduates mushroomed under decentralization. He says,

To illustrate the magnitude, in financial terms, of the opportunities which unfolded, it is helpful to recall that a typical starting salary, in 1948, for a college graduate was $200 per month. GE's starting rate was $225. A salary of $8,000 or $9,000 would represent an ambitious lifetime goal for most college graduates of that year. The average pay of all company employees, at that time, was about $3,000. During the following fifteen years the *average* employee compensation was destined to pass the $8,000 mark, and the starting salary for a college graduate was to rise to $6,588. Enterprising executives were to be rewarded by salary levels of $30,000 and upwards in their rise through the vast new arena of middle management.[28]

Today's average income per employee (wages or salary) is over $9000.

Contrary to the preachings of decentralization, however, along with its implementation came an emphasis on conformity. Instead of developing a departmental approach to management philosophy, the departments relied heavily on "central intelligence." Companywide incentive plans were put into effect. A formal structure of position guides, job specifications, salary scales, and employee-rating procedures was for the first time established. Today it may seem impossible that such a giant firm should have lasted so long without these essentials, but only with the managerial revolution inside the company did they become actually developed into practice.[a] Attempts were made to install a bonus plan and control system which could reflect performance in eight key result areas. (The eight key result areas will be detailed in subsequent chapters. They are: Profitability, Market Position, Productivity, Product Leadership, Personnel Development, Employee Attitudes, Public Responsibility, and Balance Between Short-Range Goals and Long-Range Goals.)

Chains of command were established with clearly defined channels of communications. Management courses were set up to inculcate the new concept of decentralization. Even top level management, as well as third and fourth level, went to school at the company's Crotonville, New York complex where Drucker, Dale, Argyris, Haire, Brooks, and others were frequent instructors at the old Harry Hopf estate.[29] "Two-way" communications received emphasis. The interdependence and the significance of authority, responsibility, and accountability were thoroughly developed, especially by the outstanding mind of Harold F. Smiddy and his Management Consultation Services Division. Regular reviews of results were conducted and an organized reporting system was established.

Managerial positions multiplied under decentralization, and to combat the manpower need the company appealed to self-development, thus developing the firm's concept of self-control. The firm believed that each manager must be able to evaluate himself, to be able to measure himself, using the same measuring devices as his superior would use. This concept is called self-control by GE managers, and today we understand that this was the first use of Management By Objectives in practice. The results of this self-evaluation should be evident before the same conclusion can be drawn by his superior. Even with the self-development concept the philosophy continued to charge each manager with a responsibility for the development of subordinates. The decentralization reorganization needed so many new managers that management talent became more of a premium than it was before Cordiner. Yet it was under Cordiner that the firm first developed the three-deep concept—that is, the firm likes to have three candidates for each potential opening in any three-year period.[30] The stated principles of self-development and self-control include:

1. Development is primarily the responsibility of the individual himself.
2. Manpower development is based on helping the individual to do his present job better—"Our best way of getting a promotion is to deliver outstanding results on our present job."

---

[a]In defense of General Electric it must be remembered that few companies during the 1950s had any of these management tools. By 1955 GE was academically at the forefront of American business in terms of the managerial tools used for the formal structure.

3. Learning on the job is more important and more effective than learning by study and educational courses. "We can't learn to swim without getting wet."

4. Responsibility for the development of men is part of each manager's job.

5. The outstanding specialist has a responsibility to teach and develop the men around him.

6. A sound manpower program should be designed to help everyone develop to his maximum capacity: it should not be designed to help only the chosen few.

7. Manpower development plans must operate for and through the decentralized components.

8. The skills required for General Electric work can be learned and taught.[31]

Professor Currie, in reviewing the company's management philosophies during his tenure (1948-61), said,

One is impressed with their breadth of scope and their heavy reliance on the tenets of "scientific management" as developed originally by H.L. Gantt, Harry Hopf, and Frederick W. Taylor, as long ago as 1885. The injection of human relations emphasis by the Gilbreths and Mary Parker Follett is also given recognition.[32]

By the time the decentralized philosophy was developing at GE, it was understood that "scientific management" had a number of weak spots. In Drucker's *Practice of Management*, a book which draws heavily on the author's association with Harold Smiddy and his long hours as consultant to General Electric during the conceptual years of the firm's philosophy, he notes:

Scientific Management . . . has not succeeded in solving the problem of managing worker and work. . . . It has two blind spots . . . the first . . . is the belief that . . . the individual motion [is] the essence of good work organization . . . that the human being is a machine tool. . . . The second blind spot is the "divorce of planning from doing". . . . Planning and doing are separate parts of the same job; they are not separate jobs. . . . There is no work that can be performed effectively unless it contains elements of both.[33]

It should be remembered that by 1950, and the years of formulation of the decentralized management philosophy, the prevailing schools of thought in management were heavily rooted in the "scientific management" school of Frederick W. Taylor, the "principles approach" of Henri Fayol, in the writings of Follett, and particularly, at GE, in the works of Harry Hopf. Follett and Hopf seem to balance the "scientific," "principles," and "relations" approaches, for their times. With the human relations experiments of Mayo and Roethlisberger and the publication of Chester I. Barnard's *Functions of the Executive* in 1938, a new movement stressing human relations and behavioral science was launched.[34] Inside General Electric it was Harold F. Smiddy who conceptualized the balancing of the various approaches into the corporate philosophy.

The First Decade (1947-57)

In 1947 General Electric had basically the same organization as in 1945 (Figure 2-2), extremely simple in organization structure, with only six operating departments. In December of 1950 it had ten major operating departments (Figure 2-3), with six service divisions. This 1950 organization chart was the *first* overall organization chart made widely known in the history of the company[35]—Swope did not believe in them. In January 1951 Cordiner jarred the organization by beginning a two-year shakedown in organization structure, which created about two thousand new management assignments and ended up with twenty decentralized divisions containing seventy independent operating departments.[36] An operating department is a profit center, or an entire "business" unto itself, acting as if it were an independent company. The 1952 divisions were organized into five groups: affiliated and foreign companies; apparatus; industrial products and lamps; appliances and electronics; defense products.

In early 1952 *Fortune* quoted Cordiner: "All the basic change is behind us." *Fortune* commented, "Mr. Cordiner is in the habit of settling problems years ahead, and when he calls the new GE structure complete, he means complete, he means not simply for the present fifty-four departments, but for up to seventy-five."[37] But by 1956, the company's organization had mushroomed into over one hundred and fifteen decentralized and semiautonomous operating entities, arranged into twenty-two divisions and having nine more divisions of services with over sixty more departments. (No organization chart was issued in 1957. No charts were issued between July 1, 1956, and July 24, 1958.) Currie, as an employee during these changes, proudly states,

The myriad of details and major decisions which accompanied these changes represented an almost incomprehensible network of complications in facilities and manpower adjustments. The accomplishment of a depth reorganization of such awesome proportions, in a time of unprecedented expansion pressures, is a monumental tribute to its planners and executors.[38]

In 1953 Harold F. Smiddy's staff completed an intensive study of management development—a nineteen-volume, eleven-hundred-page report believed to be the best synthesis of information yet prepared on the subject.[39] In 1954 the company led the way by setting up a department of Operations Research and Synthesis under Smiddy and headed by Mel Hurni—today one of the most respected names in the field.[40]

By 1952, sales had reached $2.6 billion,[41] nearly double the volume of 1947. In 1953, a ten-year forecast was made which called for a goal of $4 billion in sales for 1962 ($4 billion was reached in 1956, just three years later).[42] The 1954 forecast was a projection of more rapid growth, expecting $5 or $7 or

23

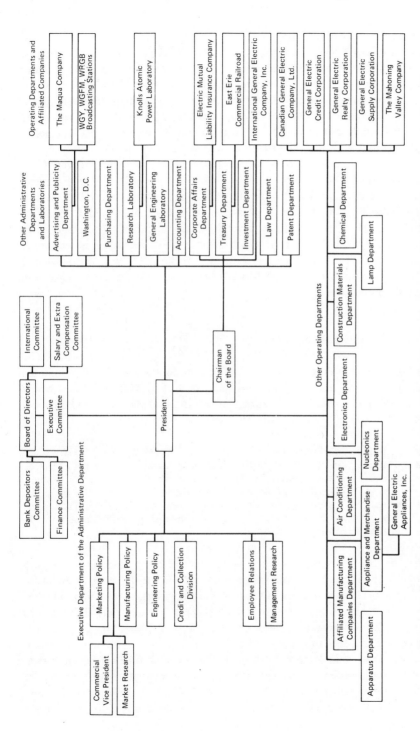

Figure 2-3. 1950 Organizational Chart (First Official Chart). Source: *Professional Management in General Electric Book One: General Electric's Growth* (New York: General Electric Company, 1953), fig. 16.

perhaps even $9 billion in 1963.[43] This did not appear to be unrealistic in view of the growth of 1947-53, an increase from $1.3 billion to $3.1 billion. The year 1963 turned out to have $4.9 billion,[44] and even 1969, with $8.4 billion, failed to reach $9 billion.[45] The 1972 figure for sales was $10.4 billion.[46]

At General Electric, the Chairman of the Board is usually subordinate to the President. At the outset of 1958, Cordiner promoted himself to Chairman and moved Robert Paxton to President. When Cordiner became Chairman the power position moved with him; the Chairman was superior to the President. In fact, Cordiner created another post, which he also put himself in, called Chief Executive Officer. The real power position at GE is the post of Chief Executive Officer. When Paxton was unable to ride out the antitrust storm in 1961, he gave up the presidency to Gerald L. Phillippe, who later succeeded Cordiner as Chairman in 1963, yet Phillippe never held the number one position. When Cordiner resigned in 1963, Fred Borch became the power when he was made President. Phillippe continued as Chairman. Technically, Borch handled the operating divisions and Phillippe handled services.[47] But the power reigned in operations, not services.

Growth Again Under Borch (1964-70)

Fred Borch became President of GE just fifteen months after he was promoted to Executive Vice President (a post originally offered to Smiddy).[48] In the only interview he has granted since retirement, Cordiner explained how Borch was chosen.

I told the Board, you know, we're going to have to make a change pretty soon, because I'm not going to stay here til I'm sixty-five. I gave them a list of fifteen fellows whose ages were right. . . . They averaged about forty-three, or something like that. Some of them were in their thirties. Then I cut the list down until we had five. I went over it very carefully with the Board. . . . They knew these fellows. I made it my business to see that they did. It finally came down to three, and then Fred Borch was chosen.[49]

One of Borch's early moves was to reshape some divisions. This was incorrectly interpreted by many as recentralization, but it was not. The major organizational changes occurred in two of the firm's biggest revenue producers: the home appliances and electronic data processing equipment (EDP).[50] On January 1, 1966, all research, development, and production of major appliances (kitchen and laundry equipment) were reorganized into one division, known as Major Appliance and Hotpoint Division. The division still kept separate sales forces for GE-branded and Hotpoint-branded products within this division. At the same time, all EDP operations were combined into Information Systems Division. This division had control over domestic as well as foreign operations in this area, such as Olivetti-General Electric of Italy and Bull-General Electric of France. This type of organization, although new to GE, is basically the type of decentralization used in the auto industry.

One year later the first major organizational changes since the early Cordiner years were made. Again heralded as evidence of recentralization, the move was not a recentralization of the corporation.[51] Borch reorganized the top echelon by organizing a team termed the "President's Office," which was the creation of a five-man executive group similar to that of General Motors. President Borch, Chairman Phillippe, and three Executive Vice Presidents formed the President's Office. At the same time, the firm doubled its operating groups from five to ten. General Electric said,

The former top executive team was felt to be too small to provide the leadership needed for the Company's projected future growth. This expansion at the group level is being implemented by increasing the components at the division level from twenty-nine to forty-seven, and by the formation of some forty new product departments.[52]

The expansion of top level management was pushed forth because of the company's expanding market after 1963. The company, after the plateau period, 1957-68, was able to boost sales by over 60 percent in the five years after 1963.[53] The reorganization gave top management more flexibility, as the top quintet was concerned with "company-wide commitments and policies that have both short- and long-term impact on GE's worldwide business."[54]

The reorganization actually carried decentralization a step further. It doubled the operating groups, increased divisions to nearly 50, and expanded the profit centers, the departments, from 110 to 150.[55] By 1969, there were 170.[56] Since 1963 General Electric had added $2.9 billion in volume, which matched the 1967 total sales of Westinghouse, the firm that came closest to being an across-the-board competitor. Borch says, "We had let things grow too big down where the work is done."[57] He reorganized the faster-growing operations, breaking them down into "pieces small enough for one man to get his arms around,"[58] Borch added, using a favorite Cordiner expression.

Cordiner moved General Electric from a $2 billion company to a $5 billion one in thirteen years. Borch in five years has led it from $5 billion to an $8-1/2 billion (value of sales made). Borch, a marketing man, increased GE's foreign volume 76 percent during the first four years after Cordiner.[59] The sales mark of $8.4 billion in 1968 more than doubled that of a decade earlier. The company has been growing at a rate of $1 billion each year for the past three years.[60] But profits did not keep pace. Earnings as a percentage of sales ranged between eight percent and five percent through the Fifties (averaging 5.9 percent).[61] During the Sixties the earnings as a percentage of sales ran between 5.7 and 4.1 percent, averaging 4.9 percent.[62] After 1963, only 1965 was above five percent, with 5.7 percent, the average for Borch and the rapidly expanding sales was only 4.7 percent.

Gerald L. Phillippe died in October of 1968. Fred Borch was promoted to Chairman of the Board. Like Cordiner before him, he took over the title of Chief Executive Officer, but he vacated the presidential title. Rumor has it that Borch was afraid of slighting one of the three Executive Vice Presidents—William H. Dennler, Jack S. Parker, and Herman L. Weiss—so no man was designated as President. All three were made Vice Chairmen.[63] Thus, the President's Office had no President, but was made up of the Chief Executive Officer and Chairman of the Board, both positions held by Borch, and the three Vice Chairmen, Dennler, Parker, and Weiss. The latter three were immediately "elected" to the Board of Directors. Borch and his triumvirate were the only inside members of the General Electric Board, consisting of twenty members. This was the organizational arrangement of General Electric at the end of the 1960s, and it remained intact until Fred Borch retired to his home in Darien, Connecticut and turned the reins of leadership over to Reginald H. Jones, currently Chairman of the Board and Chief Executive Officer.

Summary

"General Electric was fortunate to enter the most sustained growth business of the twentieth century,"[64] Cordiner once noted. At the time of its conception it was a large firm, as were most of the organizations put together by the house of Morgan near the turn of the century. Sales in the first nine months (April-December, 1892) were about $12 million; they rose to just over $20 million in 1900, and over $100 million in 1912. Five years later that was doubled, and by 1920 the firm had sales of over $300 million.[65] The Depression years saw sales dip below $200 million once, but the firm never missed a dividend. The first $1-billion sales year came during World War II, in 1943. After 1943 the firm failed to turn $1 billion in sales only once, in 1946, a year the firm suffered a nine-week plant closing caused by strike.[66] In 1951 the firm became a $2-billion company; in 1953, $3 billion; in 1956, $4 billion; in 1963, $5 billion; in 1965, $6 billion; in 1966, $7 billion; in 1968 the firm went over the $8-billion sales level, and in 1972 turned the $10-billion mark.

The growth of General Electric can easily be seen in volume of sales, or value of output, by balance sheets and profit-and-loss statements. Intangibles mingled with some tangibles caused this growth. Without the managerial minds, the organizational structure, and the spirit of the combination, General Electric would have been, to quote Owen D. Young, nothing but "a musclebound mass of mediocrity."[67] In 1963, a panel of presidents and board chairmen, 300 in number, named General Electric the best-managed company in the United States.[68] These men knew the history of the firm, its numerous antitrust suits, its labor problems; they also knew its research, leadership, and management organization. As a training ground for executive management, General Electric is perhaps outranked only by the Harvard Business School. There are so many high-ranking executives in New York alone, trained by GE but no longer working for the firm, that they have formed a club and meet once a month.[69] Paul B. Nelson, Jr., Advertising Vice President of North American Phillips, says, "There's no better training program in the world."[70] General Electric may have staffed more executive positions outside the firm than any other company, but it has also staffed its own organization well.

The Cordiner-led decentralization is similar to what other firms have since done, on paper—the organization charts are similar, but few reorganizations have worked so well. "I think that the reason decentralization hasn't worked in other companies," said Board Chairman Phillippe, "is because although many of them put out organization charts and all the other trappings, and made the right noises, they couldn't bring themselves to the point of putting a man on the spot and giving him complete responsibility."[71] The next few chapters will delve into how the company seeks to give a man complete responsibility without losing control.

3

The Philosophy and Structure of the General Electric Organization

The first part of this chapter will describe the three principal branches of the corporation: Executive (long-range planning and controlling), Services (internal consulting and advising), and Operative (producing and selling—the profit centers). The distinct separation of responsibilities of each and their relationships with each other are explained. The second part, "managerial level," explains how the firm uses a maximum of seven levels of managers between the highest-ranking officer and the lowest-ranking manager. It is important to understand that it is the third managerial level that is the famous profit-and-loss center, and therefore it is this level which has been given most final decision-making authority for each product. Part three explains why the company does not use or make provision for decision-making committees. The last part explains the absence of "assistant" or "assistant to" positions in the structure.

The Executive Office

The General Electric organization structure contains two distinct concepts which must be comprehended if the decentralization operations and control are to be understood. The first concept is the sphere of authority of the Executive, Operative, and Services branches, respectively, of the organization. The second concept involves the roles played by the successive levels of the organization, the Group, Division, and Product Department.

The first concept of the three areas of the organization—Executive, Operative, and Services—is extremely important. These three distinct categories carry clear separation of responsibilities:

1. Executive Officers are responsible principally for decisions concerning over-all company objectives and policies in the balanced best interest of all concerned with the company's present and future productivity. The executive officers do not have day-to-day operating responsibility for the company's separate product businesses.

2. Operating Managers are responsible principally for profitable execution of such objectives and policies in their particular component operating business and have complete accountability for performance and profit.

3. Services Officers, Managers, and Consultants are responsible principally for pioneering and communicating best practices in their particular functional fields, for aiding in formulation of objectives and policies, and for advising and assisting both executive officers and operating managers in all possible ways.[1]

The Executive Office is therefore responsible for a companywide view, for broad objectives, policies, and plans of the company as a whole, and for appraisal or control over the results in the interests of the various corporate publics. The evolution of the office began in 1913 when Coffin moved from the presidency to Chairman of the Board, and he and President Rice were considered as the "executive office." From time to time a powerful vice president or two, having "the ear of Number One," would be included in the "executive office," although this was informal. Under Swope, a man who built committee upon committee, the establishment of the Executive Department in 1936 was a major step in forming the Executive Office. By 1949, under Wilson, the concept was expanded so that all staff vice presidents were members of the Executive Committee. But it should be noted that from 1892 to sometime during Swope's tenure the President was both "Chief Executive Officer" and "Chief Operating Manager." During this period only the President and his immediate subordinates had profit responsibility. It was under Swope that this concept of the President having control over operations, that is, profit responsibility, was found to be unrealistic in such a large diversified operating company.[2]

Since Cordiner established the Executive Office in 1951, this Office has included the President and/or Chief Executive Officer (title used at various times since 1958),[a] Chairman of the Board, Group Executives, and Services Officers. The Executive Office was made up of all the top ranking officers from Operations and Services. Division Executives, many of whom were Vice Presidents, were not included in the Executive Office since they reported directly to a member, usually the Group Executive, an organization structure very similar to that used for the Group Vice Presidents at General Motors today. (At one time, beginning in 1951, there was a group headed by Philip Reed, Chairman of the Board, who, in turn, reported to Ralph Cordiner, President.) The company believes that this organization "represents a practical arrangement for 'lengthening the President's managerial arms' with respect to groups of Operating components without interposing a separate level in the organization structure."[3]

A short quote from Ralph Cordiner's paper presented at the General Management Conference of the American Management Association in 1952 will help to explain further this concept and why it does not, in theory, constitute another layer of management.

This "Executive Office" has been deliberately created and developed so that the top executive officers are increasingly able to free up their time to participate in planning and organizing. . . . You will observe that [the Group Executives] . . . do not constitute a "layer of management." Thus these Group Executives have "line" authority and are never to be considered as "staff" or "service" officers. The Group Executives' authority is a substitute or delegated

---

[a]The positions of President and Chief Executive Officer are distinct positions, although often held by the same man in General Electric.

type of authority with equivalent responsibility and thus accountability. Hence, these officers do not have Operating responsibility as we have defined it, but actually are Administrative or Executive Officers. The highest Operating level is that of the Division General Manager, as the full profit-making responsibility for the individual Division and Department business rests on the respective General Managers of such decentralized businesses.

Instead, the Group Executives truly are Executive Officers, aiding the President in his over-all responsibilities, but each with respect to his particular Group of product businesses as distinct from the President's Executive responsibility for the complete enterprise. They are really, therefore, an extension of the mind and arms of the President, working closely with him, familiar with his aims, plans and organization concepts; and able to speak for him and in his stead in interpreting these to the Divisional and Departmental Operating Managers within their respective Groups.

. . . each Services Officer or Group Executive so organizes his other work as to be able to set apart a measurable portion of his time during which he can act as one of this group of officers, working together with the President and thinking in terms of the Company's over-all objectives, policies, organization, management personnel, plans, budgets, controls, and performance.[4]

To the present time, none of the foregoing has been altered in the company's managerial philosophy. To some eyes, this Executive Office may appear to complicate the corporate structure. Cordiner had developed it to simplify the organization. He wanted top management to have more time to think, more time for forward planning. Before 1951 and the organization of this office, GE used forty-seven management type committees to do the work that after the reorganization was done either by two committees linked with the Executive Office or by single individuals charged with the responsibility for those decisions.[5] The two Executive Office committees were the Advisory Council and the Appropriations Committee. The Advisory Council forms broad policies; the Appropriations Committee was later abolished when a written corporate policy was developed covering capital and expense authorities. (This policy will be described later in this chapter.) Complicating the picture of the Executive Office for students of organization, General Electric, from time to time, uses two titles for those people who can act as president for particular groups. The first is the Executive Office, comprised of the Chief Executive Officer, Chairman of the Board, Operating Group Vice Presidents, and Services Officers. When acting with line authority only (when Services were not included), the group is known as the President's Office. The only difference between the Executive Office and President's Office is that the President's Office handles problems and policies that do not affect the Services; therefore, it deals only with pure line-operating policy. The old President's Office has been discontinued, but company jargon refers to the organization comprised of the Chief Executive Officer, President, and Vice Chairman as the President's Office.

Harold F. Smiddy, with Cordiner the principal designer of the Executive Office and its smaller section, the President's Office, was once asked, "Aren't you just kidding us to count it as only 'one level,' as you do, for Organization Structuring purposes?" His answer was:

In the first place, that a group that small, who dedicate themselves to doing so, can become able to work *substantially* "as one," even if they use different words and have different personalities. Now three years ago [1953] we said that was the *goal.* But at that time you could talk to one Group Executive and then another, and you'd say "nuts"; because they not only didn't sound alike but they were really saying different things.

    Today I don't think that's so. We contact those fellows about as much as any of you and we go the circuit with them and tap the most diverse problems with them and can see just how they do tick. So what do we see? Well, of course, they still have the different personalities and the different words. But there is a surprising *uniformity* in what they basically say, if you're listening, through their different phraseology and personalities. This is what I see. I think it is what you'll see *too* if you stop being pure skeptics a while and really look and really listen.

    [In the Executive Office] you do need more than one man at the helm, even if we do the best we know how to prepare any man for that responsibility and to prepare successors and so on; and it is true that the essential Executive work is so unique and at the same time so similar for each of the persons concerned that there is truly no "layer" or "level" than from an Organization Structuring standpoint.[6]

Services or Functional Components

Each operating department in General Electric has full responsibility for engineering, manufacturing, marketing, finance, personnel, and legal operations. It would be an exceptional department that did not, from time to time, encounter problems beyond the experience of its members. The Services components help to fill some of the need for specialists with depth knowledge. The company takes from operations "the most skilled, the most experienced, the most imaginative men"[7] and puts them into Services, claims Arthur Vinson, former Vice President of Manufacturing Services and later a Group Executive. He goes on:

They will not only know how to do work in their respective functions but will also know how to seek better ways and to teach them, thus advancing and multiplying availability of knowledge in each function. Once found, such men are promoted from product operating organizations and put into company-wide functional services divisions. If, on occasion, we fail to identify men of sufficient caliber for our needs in such respects, we do not hesitate to go outside of our General Electric organization in this hunt for talent.[8]

Since the 1951 Cordiner organization of the Service components there has been very little change. That was the first year of Services as organization components, and they reported to President Cordiner. The 1960 group reported to Cordiner as Chairman of the Board and Chief Executive Officer. They did not report to President Paxton, who was responsible for all operations. In 1970 the Services reported to the new President's Office. (Realistically they reported to Borch as Chief Executive Officer. See Figure 3-1).

The General Electric Services concept, new to the company in 1951, is in fact an old concept, found in the military and religion as well as in corporate organizations. General Motors used this staff concept as early as the term of Pierre S. du Pont.[9] Cordiner and Smiddy, in setting up the General Electric organization, wanted to develop the General Motors type of environment and structure. They must have been aware of what Drucker had written of General Motors in 1946—the following concept can be found in the philosophy writings of Cordiner, Smiddy, and most of the General Electric literature about the place of staff in General Electric theory.

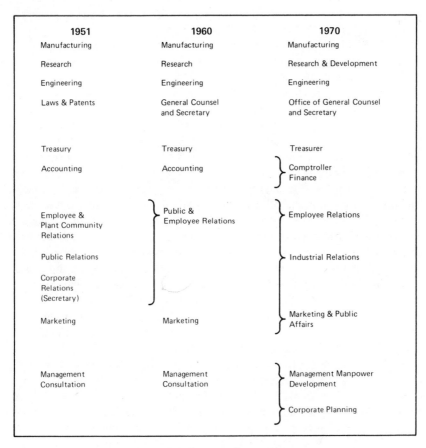

Figure 3-1. Services Components.

It should be emphasized that the staff agencies in their relations with the divisions rely on suggestions and advice, and that they have no direct authority whatsoever over the divisional manager and his policies. Of course, they might appeal to top management in a last attempt to force an obstructionist divisional manager into line; this, however, is a theoretical rather than a practical recourse. In the normal course of events the service staffs have to "sell themselves" to the divisional manager, and have to rely on their ability to convince the divisional management and on their reputation and achievements. No divisional manager is under compulsion to consult the service staff or to take their advice. Yet the relationship between service staffs and divisional managers is on the whole quite frictionless.[10]

At General Electric the Services act as the central trust or clearinghouse for all the technical and specialized areas of the business. They are the consultants for all of GE's businesses and are, as John Thackray noted in *Dun's Review*, "a strong force that keeps departments or divisions from anarchy. They have no power of command; their job is simply to question, probe, inform, or advise the department men on the front line."[11]

Gerald Phillippe, as President, once said, "The question of how you hold together a company when it's decentralized is a very serious problem. Our services are the mortar that holds the company together."[12] These service organizations are deliberately designed to act as social innovators; that is, they are specifically organized to systematically diagnose social needs and opportunities and to develop concepts and designs to satisfy them. Drucker said in 1959 that General Electric was the only company he knew of that set up its headquarter service organizations to deliberately act as social innovators.[13]

Services do not carry line authority in Operating components. The authority of people in Services and any person outside his own component is indirect. Authority comes from the influence of suggestions and persuasion, and from the "authority of knowledge," expertness. It comes from advising and teaching in the functional field of particular expertise. The Services "authority" comes from keeping ahead in theory and method of the particular function, pioneering in knowledge, if need be. Services are also responsible for developing and coordinating the firm's national and international associationships and relationships in each functional field. Within each functional field (Services), each separate Service component is responsible for "doing any company-wide Operating work which, by its corporate or over-all nature, cannot be performed naturally and effectively in decentralized Operating components."[14]

Traditionally, only a few activities have fallen into this category of operating functions that have not been decentralized but are in Services components at General Electric: basic types of general research, general engineering development, consolidated accounting, institutional advertising, and union relations, which are so required by contract.[15] This kind of work found in Services has been called "pooled operating work," so as not to confuse the philosophy of the structure.

The Services also are responsible for doing some "operating work for which specific Operating components wish to contract for and pay for."[16] This intracompany charging is rarer today than it was during the first few years after reorganization. William Greenwood, Consultant in Management Consultation Services for a decade under Smiddy, said,

When I was in General Electric we were the only Services component that really did charge, and we did it for maybe only a couple of years. I think Management Consultation Services, which was the name of our division under Smiddy, was able to do this because of the great need for knowledge in the whole field of organization.[17]

Becoming more specific, he continued,

As I recall, Smiddy's time went something like $500 a day—which, going back into 1952 to 1953 was pretty damn high! I forget what [Paul] Mills' was, but I think it was $250 a day, and I think mine was only $100 a day. But that's plus expenses. Expenses, of course, means travel, living, entertainment, and things of that kind. Nobody objected to the payment, but it could have been out of fear of what might have happened. . . . Smiddy was in favor of charging for the services on the grounds that if you're any good they come to you. So far as to what the competition was charging at that time, well, those were the days when we were only paying Drucker about $250 a day.

This type of billing or charging for services did not last long. In fact, Smiddy didn't even remember doing it when questioned on this subject about fifteen years later. Greenwood, questioned as to why this billing was given up, replied:

I'm not too sure, except that I have strong impressions that nobody would ask us to do anything for them if they were going to be billed specifically. Since we wouldn't have any work, the chances are that no matter what objectives we had set for ourselves . . . nobody wanted us. I am quite sure that would leave a distasteful image in the eyes of the chief executive [Cordiner]. So, Smiddy, very wisely, decided at that particular time [1953] that he wouldn't charge them either. On the other hand, once our time was charged out as an assessment against the total corporation, requests were so heavy that Smiddy had to increase his component by about ten times.

Services are considered to be of higher status in the organization structure than are operations of similar title. For instance, a man moving from the position of Operating Department General Manager to Services Manager would be receiving a promotion in status and in compensation. The companywide Services involve greater responsibility and carry a greater possible impact on the performance of the whole company than do the operating positions at corresponding levels.[18] This higher status for Services work was later to cause a personnel problem, which will be discussed below.

The thirteen-page "Services Officer Position Guide" gives a more complete understanding of the total concept of Services work. Quoting from the opening paragraph, the broad function is that:

The Services Officer has Executive Officer and Services responsibilities. He is responsible for Executive, Managerial, and Functional types of work, and for Services Functional and Appraisal work. He is accountable to the Chairman of the Board and Chief Executive Officer for the efficient managing of the Services component, and for the quality of Services Functional and Appraisal work.[19]

The "Services Officer Position Guide" then goes on to detail the generic responsibilities, authority, and accountabilities for the position under the four broad functions: services functional and appraisal work, executive work, managerial work, and functional work (operating). Figure 3-2 summarizes the generic responsibilities common to all services work. These responsibilities are built into each specific Position Guide.

To detail the work of the service organizations, a close look at one of the services is of some benefit. Marketing Services performs its function just as the other services perform theirs. The company by 1970 was organized into about one hundred and seventy separate product departments, each with a general manager, marketing manager, engineering manager, financial manager, and manufacturing manager. Each department has a clearly defined scope of products and markets to be served. The marketing manager is expected to perform a major role in the preparation of business plans for his department. These business plans must reflect the company's budget objectives of volume, profit, and other aspects of the eight key result areas, to be explained in greater detail in Chapter 4. Although the products of some departments—mainly industrial components and "apparatus"—are sold jointly,[20] decentralization has

---

Managers and Consultants in Services work have the following fundamental and generic companywide responsibilities with respect to their particular subfunction; namely to

1. Study, seek and know functional principles and the best practices that have been developed either outside or inside the company.

2. Develop professional expertness and deserve and earn recognition outside and inside the company.

3. Contribute to the advancement of fundamental knowledge; and invent, pioneer, develop, and formulate better principles and practices.

4. Design and recommend pertinent patterns, systems, classifications, and nomenclature.

5. Develop, recommend, and interpret functional objectives, policies, and plans.

6. Provide clearinghouse service; and communicate and teach functional principles, theories, philosophies, and practices.

7. Measure, review, and appraise present practices as requested or needed.

8. Cooperate in voluntary teamwork toward the achievement of company objectives.

9. Lead and teach by persuasion, example, and the authority of knowledge.

10. Practice and encourage "business statesmanship."

Figure 3-2. Generic Responsibilities Common to all Services Work. Source: *Professional Management in General Electric Book Two: General Electric's Organization* (New York: General Electric Company, 1955), p. 131.

created more than one hundred clearly defined marketing manager positions in the company. These positions are in operating management and are not in or under the control of Marketing Services.

Then the question arises, where does Marketing Services fit, and what does it do? Fred Borch, long-time head of Marketing Services before becoming President, once said part of its job is long-range corporate marketing thinking and planning. As a member of the Executive Office, it advises the Board and top managers.[21] Marketing Services also introduces and helps supervise corporate marketing policies. Borch emphasized in 1958, "Actually, however, the number of policies has been reduced sharply in the last five years. Only three have been added: on internal pricing, continued use of affiliated companies' trademarks, and on the sale of company products to employees."[22]

General Electric does not have a company overall pricing policy or resale policy. Each operating department has complete control over pricing its own products. Although it is not company policy, some departments "fair-trade" their products; some do not. Speaking on the subject of corporate marketing policy, Borch said, "When we think that a new policy is needed, it is worked out on the services level only *after* we've obtained the opinions of operating management about it."[23]

Advertising is carried on by both Operating departments and Services. When advertising is developed to sell a particular product, known at GE as "sales" advertising, it is an operations function and Marketing Services counsels but cannot direct the sales campaign. A department has the right to reject all of the counseling, and if a department does not ask for counseling it will not receive any. Institutional advertising, on the other hand, is carried on by the Marketing Services. General Electric spends more money institutionally, advertising "GE," than all the operating departments spend collectively.

Marketing Services was originally set up in the 1951 organization plan. Originally the objectives were

to assist the President, Group Executives and Operating Management to obtain maximum sales volume and profits by helping to formulate over-all marketing objectives, policies and plans; providing marketing services, advice and counsel; conducting audits of effectiveness, economy, and efficiency of marketing performance; creating good customer relations, and promoting the usefulness and interchange of marketing information.[24]

These objectives have expanded and are stated in both long- and short-range terms, reflecting the eighth key area of measurements. (The eight key result areas are discussed in Chapter 4.) The following can be found as Marketing Services objectives:

Long-Range:
To assure that marketing will [help to] guide the company toward its growth and profit goals.

That policies, strategies and practices anticipate, and be compatible with, our constantly evolving social, economic and political environments.

To acquire, develop, and communicate the type of knowledge which will help raise the standards of marketing performance.

Short-Range:

To understand operating situations. Communicate existing knowledge and develop new knowledge to help operating units to do a better marketing job.

To help to sense opportunities for cooperative activities among them, and to help in translating these opportunities into action.[25]

Most of the other services are organized similarly to Marketing Services. Marketing Services has research specialists who develop new knowledge about the company and its environment which should help in making marketing decisions. There are consultants who act as liaisons between Operations and Marketing Services. There are also "Marketing Specialization Consultants," who are aides to operating components on particular functions of marketing, such as marketing research, product planning, advertising, and sales promotion, and even on organization planning and nomenclature.[26] Marketing Services has organized a section that is concerned with marketing personnel development and recruitment. This part of the organization works with operations to help them on their manpower planning and development. It conducts college recruitment programs and runs training programs. The training programs are run only if a company-wide program is the most effective method or if a department particularly requests such a program. It holds Advanced Marketing Seminars and has produced a basic training course. "On request supplies names of individuals for specific openings."[27] The Advanced Marketing Seminars, conducted five times a year, are four weeks long. Two weeks are spent at the seminar center, two weeks back on the job, and the final two weeks back at the center. Usually twenty students per class are selected from men nominated by division managers. The instructors come from within the company and from colleges. In 1958, one of the first years of the program, nineteen college professors were used, including D. Maynard Phelps of Michigan and E. Raymond Corey of Harvard.[28] These seminars are not to be confused with the companywide Crotonville School, which will be discussed later. Three-day workshops relating to specific topics are organized at the request of a division or department.

Like the other services, Marketing Services, in theory, is not supposed to initiate changes. One member once said, "We'd be glad, of course, to pass leads along, but usually we don't run into them."[29] All the Services are expected to make suggestions, but only after they have been asked for them. Services do not normally initiate. If Marketing Services believes a change should be made in operations, it has two courses of action available to it: it can counsel the operating department and can try to "sell" its idea, or the head of Marketing Services can send the suggestion to the Group Executive. If the Group Executive accepts it, the suggestion goes through the Division Manager to the Department

Manager. This is how it works in the corporate theory; the problem with the implementation of the theory is left for discussion in Chapter 5.

Operating Components

The decentralized businesses are found in the Operating components. This is, perhaps, the heart of decentralization. The Operating components are responsible for salable products and customer services. Cordiner said that each Operating component has responsibility for engineering, manufacturing, and marketing, "each of them bearing full operating responsibility and authority for the Company's success and profitability in a particular product or service field."[30] The Operating components have line authority and a division or department general manager is, philosophically, a "president" of a decentralized product Operating business. The Operating departments are grouped by similarities to form divisions, and these divisions are combined to form eleven operating groups. (This will be further detailed in the description of the layers of organization.) The heads of the Operating groups are members of the Executive Office. By 1970 there were eleven groups, up from the basic five found throughout most of the 1950s. With the elimination of Information Systems the total was reduced to ten. The groups in General Electric have been:[31]

1952	*1960*	*1970*
1. Affiliated and Foreign Companies	1. Consumer Product	1. Aerospace
2. Apparatus	2. Electric Utility	2. Aircraft Engine
3. Industrial Products Company	3. Electronic, Atomic and Defense Systems	3. Appliance and Television
4. Appliance and Electronics	4. Industrial	4. Components and Materials
5. Defense Products	5. International	5. Construction Industries
		6. Consumer Products
		7. Industrial
		8. Information Systems
		9. International
		10. Power Generation
		11. Power Transmission and Distribution

The Operating departments are the basic "businesses," the building blocks on which the whole decentralization scheme rests. Each Operating department is a profit center. There are over one hundred and sixty departments today. Above the department level is the division level, which coordinates the activities and needs of the many "businesses" which have similarities, enabling them to be organized into a particular division; currently there are approximately fifty divisions. Above this level is the Executive layer, headed by the ten Group Vice Presidents. About 98 percent of the employees of the company work in these Operating components at one level or another.[32] The departments are reasonably autonomous "businesses" and are charged with profit responsibility. Therefore, each department has been assigned corresponding authority over all the functions that affect the results, because GE feels that without this authority a manager could not fairly be held accountable for profits. The minimum requirements needed to develop an autonomous "business" status for an Operating department are, according to Smiddy:

(a) That it have *both a distinct product line* (or for a non-manufacturing business, a distinct and salable *service*) *and a distinct market* (or customer identity); and

(b) That its *"manager"* have both *authority* and *responsibility* for all of those basic *functional kinds of work* really essential to determine *profit results*; which, as a minimum, need to be those concerned with the *"distinct product"* and *"distinct market"* characteristics or specifically with applicable "engineering" (including development) and "marketing" work and, where involved, the attendant "manufacturing" (including purchasing), "employee relations," and "finance" (specifically, cash and credit, as distinct from accounting) work.[33]

As "autonomous" businesses the Operating departments have broad objectives written into each General Manager's position guide. From these broad objectives, specific objectives can be derived by the General Manager himself, with "persuasion veto power" in the division manager's office. These specific objectives will define what the business component is to accomplish, as well as what it is to provide through what sales channels for what customers in what markets, in what product lines, with what resources, and with what scope of actions and functions. The corporate philosophy stipulates that department general managers design their own specific objectives, which fit into the broad, general objectives of the product group. This philosophy can be overturned by the personalities of the managers involved. Strong-willed division managers can and perhaps do run roughshod over weaker-willed department general managers. This is contrary to the organization philosophy and can cause decentralization on paper to be centralization in reality. This problem will be discussed in more detail in Chapter 5.

Each department general manager has the authority and responsibility to determine the organization plan for his component to meet the objectives.

Within the framework of the broad objectives—which are found in the position guide, the department's function guides, and the "business charter of the department"—the general manager plans for new product lines, for expansion, for attaining a leading position, and for other changes of importance. He has the responsibility for success or failure in the eight key areas that are used to measure his effectiveness.

From the broad and specific objectives—broad objectives are top-down goals, and specific objectives are developed at the general-manager level—each general manager must determine what work needs to be done and how to get it done.[34]

Decentralization at General Electric is more than the geographic, product, or functional decentralization popular before 1950. It is much more decentralization of responsibility—the delegation of the decision-making to the lowest possible level—the lowest level at which knowledge to make the decisions allows authority to be placed. This is what shocked General Electric managers when Cordiner first put forth his plan.[35] It was an attempt to put into practice the principle of "authority to decide must be brought as closely as possible to the point where action originates,"[36] which is one of Harry A. Hopf's guides to organization.

Ralph Cordiner, in an effort to show how low the delegated authority was placed at General Electric, wrote in 1956:

To demonstrate that the responsibility, authority, accountability of these Operating Departments is real, not window dressing, consider their pricing authority. The price of a product can be raised or lowered by the managers of the Department producing it, with only voluntary responsibility on their part to give sensible consideration to the impact of such price changes on other Company products.

As further evidence of the freedom provided by decentralization to the Operating Departments, consider the fact that the operating budget of the General Electric Company is not a document prepared by the Executive Offices in New York. It is an addition of the budgets prepared by the Operating Department General Managers, with the concurrence of the Division General Managers and Group Executives. These budgets include planned sales volume, product development plans, expenditures for plant and equipment, market targets, turnover of investment, net earnings, projected organization structure, and other related items.[37]

Because the department level was responsible for profits, each department head was given almost total authority in his area. In many situations, this gave him independence for performance from those above him. The final evaluation of projects and directions taken by a department head was measured by superiors; nonetheless, a department head could go in a direction not desired by his immediate superior, for it is the department head who has final authority for the direction of his department. His forecasting ability or his judgment would be measured at a later date. A decision unpopular with a superior might turn out to be a "stroke of genius" later on. Gerald Phillippe often told two success stories of department managers making decisions which ran contrary to what the corporate leaders recommended:

Years back, one of our department heads wanted to build an electric toothbrush; everybody he talked to said he was out of his cottonpickin' mind.

Anybody too lazy to brush his teeth, by gosh, hadn't ought to be alive anyway.

He said, "All right, just give me the money to go into production, and we will see who is right."

You can guess who was right; in the first two years we sold over a million units.

I am one of those who had told him he was crazy.

Another example is the portable dishwasher. Every member of the then-existing Executive Office told that department general manager he was crazy to bring out a portable dishwasher, because we had had one before and it flopped.

But, he said, "This one is square; the other was round. This one is automatic; the other was manual."

He brought it out, and it was the best selling item we had the next three or four years.[38]

Operating components as holders of line authority may encounter the oft-voiced problem of not having real authority, as opposed to theoretical authority, often found in the staff or Services components. Chapter 5 will discuss this point in greater detail; it is sufficient here to point out the philosophy of the independence of the Operating department in General Electric. At the General Electric Group Executive Management Conference in 1952, it was carefully explained that the President and Group Executives supply leadership for the firm as a whole; Services components supply specialized advice and interpret policies; and Operating management has the responsibility for direct day-to-day operations. Whereupon the following question, "You mean these Services Divisions can't tell an Operating department what to do? I've heard there are some things we're doing because we've got to—orders from New York!"

The reply was made by one of the Group Executive Vice Presidents:

If you heard that, it probably means that somebody is lacking in intestinal fortitude. If an Operating Manager has good reasons for not accepting the advice of a Services Division, he doesn't have to do so. He is accountable for results, not the Services Division. But if he does accept the advice, he should make it his own policy and back it to the hilt. Let's cut out this buck-passing "orders-from-New-York" malarky! Now obviously, there are certain matters—such as Company wide labor relations, certain aspects of public relations and legal matters affecting corporate structure of operations—where we must have a common front, with policies recommended by the Services Divisions and approved by the President.[39]

Further questioning indicated concern over what would happen if an Operating manager refused to accept recommendations from New York or Services. The Group Executive replied that recommendations are made directly from the Services component to the Operating manager, and that the Division and Group Executives would not be involved. But, he said,

In case of a serious dispute, I might have to resolve it with the Services and Operating Managers. Or, if the Services Officer feels that the decision is one involving the interest of the Company as a whole, he can go with the Group Executive to the President.[40]

The Managerial Levels

General Electric has a maximum of seven levels of management; six levels is normal, and five is the goal. The maximum of seven counts the Chief Executive Officer (or President) and Group Executive as the highest level. The second level is the Division General Manager, and level three is the Department General Manager. So there is only one managerial level between the top level and the profit center or business level in the organization. Figure 3-3 shows the seven possible managerial levels. In each department three to five organizational levels are normally found. The Department General Manager is the top level; level two is made up of functional managers; level three (and four and five, if needed) is made up of component managers or supervisors; and the lowest level is the individual contributor employee. The individual contributor is defined by General Electric as the member of the organization who

makes his contribution to the Company's total output of goods and services through work done directly by his own personal efforts, whether as a researcher, engineer, salesman, artisan, specialist, expert, advisor, consultant, professional, or as a clerical or manual worker of any kind, in any function or branch of the total business.[41]

He is not a manager. The principal responsibility of a manager, on the other hand, is getting work done through other people. Both the manager and the individual contributor work with other people, but the former is primarily responsible for securing results through the work of others, while the latter is measured in terms of his own personal output and productivity in his particular work field.

The second level is the division. Related divisions form the groups. A division is composed of related operating departments having related and usually similar types of products, markets, or functions and for which overall operating managerial responsibility is assigned to a general manager. An example is:

Aerospace Group

Divisions:

Aircraft Equipment Division
Defense Programs Division
Electronic Systems Division
Re-entry and Environmental Systems Division
Space Division

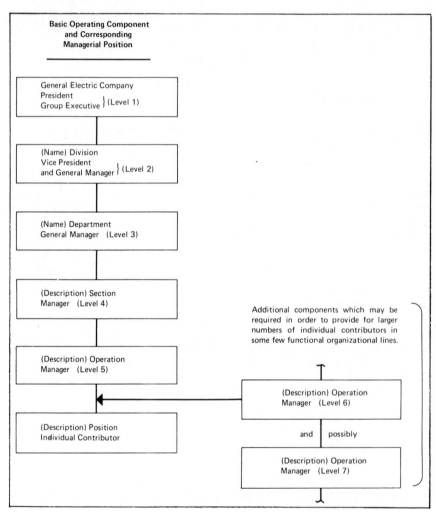

Figure 3-3. Operating Component Names and Organizational Levels. Source: *Professional Management in General Electric Book Two: General Electric's Organization* (New York: General Electric Company, 1955), p. 164.

The third level is that of the Department General Manager, who reports directly to the Division General Manager. Primarily this is the component representing a product or salable service having direct accountability for profits. An example is:

Aerospace Group
Electronic Systems Division
  Departments:
    Power Tube Department
    Receiving Tube Department
    Rectifier Components Department
    Semiconductor Products Department

The number of levels through the General Manager of the Department level is three. Within the department level there may be two or three levels between the General Manager and the individual contributor, making a total of five or six levels above the individual contributor. Before reorganization, General Electric had seventeen or eighteen layers in several divisions.[42] Peter Drucker claims, "Any business that needs more than six or seven levels between rank-and-file employee and top management [vice president level?] is too big."[43] Smiddy responded as follows to a question as to why General Electric has a goal of five managerial levels above the worker in the organization:

We have departmental businesses as small as five or six million dollars . . . others where business runs up well over a hundred million dollars annually. . . . In the first place, I don't think there's anything sacred about five. . . . How did five get into the act? It came from taking a look at the problems of trying to get an optimum balance of spans and levels as the two Organization Structure design factors that influence, on the one hand, the best integrating and communicating and, on the other hand, the best achievement of actual performance of the particular work. Five came about by looking at where we were and seeing what might be a sound goal to shoot at. We knew that seventeen or eighteen layers . . . was too many for the reason that many levels factually prevented good two-way communications.[44]

Later, Paul Mills, who helped to design the organizational structure, added that you don't organize from the top down.

You need to start out with the actual work and with the people to do it from the bottom, and go on *up*. Forget the handles that they have on these levels; whether they are general managers, general foremen or what. Start at the bottom, the worker; go up and then see how many managerial levels you need for different kinds of managing work in depth and scope.[45]

Below the department level there may be a section level, but this is not general. A section is a component within a department which in itself has a product or salable service and has accountability for profits. The section manager reports to the Department General Manager. Usually, a section is organized when the department develops a product that is similar to its generic product, but can stand alone. An example of this is sycachome, which is really a plastic but has unique qualities so that it seems to be a distinct product. Frequently, these sections grow to a point where they can be spun off as separate departments. During the maturing stages the product development will be managed as a section, until such time as the department and division manager deem it proper to organize it as a department.

Usually the next level below the Department General Manager, the fourth level, is that of the functional managers, such as Manager—Marketing, Home Laundry Department, or Manager—Finance, Home Laundry Department. Below these functional managers is the lowest managerial level which has been termed supervisory level, such as General Foreman. Reporting to this last managerial level are the individual contributors, such as auditors, procedures analysts, drill press operators, machinists, and so forth. A department would be set up as shown in Figure 3-4.

Committees

In the foregoing discussions of the organization structure of the General Electric Company, it is worth knowing that there are no provisions for the use of committees as decision-making bodies, such as those found in General Motors.

In *Professional Management in General Electric*, Harold Smiddy developed the philosophy of management issued under Ralph Cordiner's name as the official philosophy of the firm's top management. Soon after the release of this four-volume work many top executives found innumerable areas of disagreement with the philosophy, but Cordiner and Smiddy planned to persuade all to their philosophy. The *Professional Management* series was meant not only to set down on paper the corporate philosophy but to be used as a guide on how to manage, to help further the study of management, and to help organize the investigation of the area so as to upgrade the philosophy through greater in-depth reasoning.

Smiddy developed sixteen principles relating to the process of delegation, reprinted as Figure 3-5. The fifth principle explains why General Electric does not have decision-making committees: "Responsibility, like authority, is personal and cannot be shared by a group of individuals or a committee. Confusion results if this is attempted."[46]

The corporate philosophy is that committees cannot be responsible for making decisions. This conclusion is drawn from the belief that decisions are acts of mind and will, and only individuals have mind and will. Nor can a committee

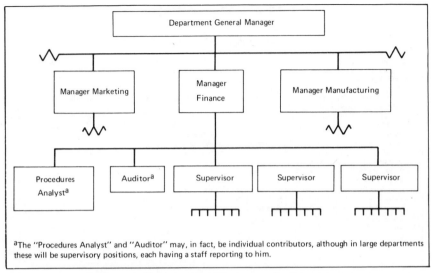

Figure 3-4. Organization Structure of a Department.

effectively be held accountable for results. The process of delegation between a manager and another individual involves responsibility and accountability as two aspects of that process. Committees cannot be held accountable for results; thus, the delegation of responsibility must be from one individual to another, as is clearly stated in the General Electric philosophy.[47] This does not rule out committees as advisory organizations.

The elimination of decision-making committees in the early 1950s was one of the most significant changes in the General Electric philosophy under Cordiner. Under Wilson and under Swope, the General Electric Company was a committee-oriented organization. When Cordiner studied the reorganization of the company he decided that he was, quite obviously, going to decentralize; but he hadn't concentrated on what this would do to committees as part of the philosophy and structure. It was not Cordiner, but Smiddy, who developed the original thinking on this subject.[48] Harold Smiddy was quite vehement in his belief that committees produced a weak organization because of the inability to pin responsibility for decision-making on any one incumbent of a position. He felt that you could not share responsibilities; that shared responsibilities promoted the weakest kind of decisions.

After Cordiner accepted this philosophy, he formalized it, and it was included in the *Professional Management* books[49] written by Smiddy and his staff. Thus, all decision-making committees were abolished. Immediately, there was an outcry by a number of managers that the Advisory Council was nothing more

Two-Way Understanding Is Required

1. Assigning responsibility for work and teamwork, transferring authority, and accepting corresponding accountability are three inseparable, complementary parts of the process of *delegation* of work. They are not separate, independent concepts.
2. Being complementary parts of one process, such responsibility, authority, and accountability are bounded by the same limits in time and in scope and are evaluated in the same units of measurement. They are simultaneous, co-terminous, and commensurate.
3. The responsibilities, authorities, and accountabilities inherent in each position in an organization structure are detailed in its "Position Guide," in order that they may be clearly understood by all concerned. Responsibilities so defined include both duty and relationships—that is, both "work" and "teamwork"—responsibilities. A team, unlike a committee, has assigned positions and *individual* responsibilities for both work and teamwork.
4. These represent a "meeting of the minds," and working understanding and arrangements, between two individuals only—a man and the manager to whom he reports.
5. Responsibility, like authority, is personal and cannot be shared by a group of individuals or a committee. Confusion results if this is attempted.
6. The definition of the areas of responsibility must be clear, precise, and complete so as to avoid confusion, omissions, or overlaps. If there is to be assurance that the work will get done, each area must be assigned by a manager to an individual, who in turn understands and accepts accountability for performance.

The Man's Part

7. The incumbent of a particular position automatically accepts the obligation of accountability to his manager for performance of all responsibilities—all duties and relationships—assigned to him when he accepts a particular position, and as long as he holds it.
8. When the incumbent of a particular position voluntarily accepts the obligation and the accountability for carrying out the defined responsibilities—for both work and teamwork—inherent in that position, he is automatically endowed with the authority which goes with the position as so designed, and which is needed to do the designated work. Such authority is inherent in the position in the organization structure. It is a mantle worn by the incumbent as long as, but only as long as, he occupies the position.
9. An individual should have only one boss, the manager to whom he reports.

The Manager's Part

10. The manager, to whom the incumbent of a particular position reports, assigns the designated responsibilities and relationships, transfers from his own position to the position of the men who report to him all authority needed to do the designated work, and rightfully expects accountability for performance of such assigned responsibilities and relationships.
11. An individual has a responsibility or he does not have it. An attempt to assign partial responsibility does not work. Partial responsibility is confusion.
12. Authority cannot be transferred and retained at the same time. An attempt to transfer partial authority does not work. Partial authority is confusion.
13. Limits to and boundaries of responsibility and relationships, of authority, and of accountability are set by the manager, and need to be co-terminous with each other.
14. To allow for maximum individual initiative, limits to or boundaries of responsibility and authority should be as broad as possible. Those necessary to achieve unity of action in the overall balanced best, or common, interests of all concerned should be stated clearly, and preferably in writing so as to avoid misunderstandings and to permit working together to achieve the corresponding common purposes.
15. Within such designated limits and boundaries, the process of delegation and each of its inseparable parts must be clear-cut, complete, and understood if delegation is to be effective and the needed work and teamwork is to be accomplished.
16. Delegating responsibility for an area of work to a man who reports to him does not relieve the manager from the responsibility for being sure that the work gets done. If the man to whom the work was delegated failed in its performance, the manager must assume the blame since his act of delegation did not relieve him of his own accountability for getting the work done. Delegation is not abdication.

Figure 3-5. Delegation: The Process of Establishing Working Agreements Between a Man and the Manager to Whom He Reports in an Organization Structure. Source: *Professional Management in General Electric Book Two: General Electric's Organization* (New York: General Electric Company, 1955), p. 95.

than a decision-making committee. The Advisory Council, one of the two Executive Office committees mentioned earlier, is just a committee to advise the President or Chief Executive Officer (Cordiner during the fifties). Cordiner answered the perplexed managers about the status of the Advisory Council:

When it comes to policy decisions, discussed at the Advisory Council, I make the decisions. But I am not so stupid that I will not listen to pros and cons. But, they could be all against me. I will still make the decision. It is my decision to make. I won't depend on a vote to determine whether or not we will do this, that, or the other thing. But, I want to get the benefit of everyone's counsel. And there is a difference between advisory [thinking] and decision-making. When I have the responsibility I will accept it.[50]

Later Cordiner wrote:

General Electric structure has no place for committees as decision-making bodies. It is my feeling that a committee moves at the speed of its least informed member, and too often is used as a way of sharing responsibility. Before decentralization, an official tried to get on a great number of committees. He would lead a very calm, safe, orderly life. Not much would happen, but nothing would ever happen to him.

Today [1956], a committee may be helpful as an advisory group, and indeed the Executive Office of the General Electric Company meets twice monthly as an Advisory Council for the President. In any such arrangement, however, it must be made abundantly clear that the authority for any particular decision lies with the responsible individual, even if he makes it while sitting with the other Council members.[51]

One other committee was very powerful at the outset of the decentralization program—the Appropriations Committee, which passed on the advisability of providing large expense or capital funds to the various operating components. Detailed documents written in the form of appropriation proposals were sent to this committee. The material was always furnished by the financial staff of the division, which was responsible for requesting the money. The Manufacturing Services component was especially powerful, as it would, with the aid of representatives of other Services, make the decision on the proposed appropriation. Harold Smiddy pointed out to Ralph Cordiner that this was in fact a decision-making committee and as such was in violation of the corporate philosophy against the use of decision-making committees. The Appropriations Committee was, therefore, abolished and was replaced by a very strong policy approved by Cordiner and issued over his name on what the authorizations would be to the various divisions, what they had to do, and how much approval in dollars would be made at each level. It was found that most of the appropriations that had gone to the Appropriations Committee could be handled at the local level, thus increasing decentralization. The larger dollar requests, which were not many, were reserved for Cordiner and the Board of Directors, but these money amounts were spelled out very specifically.

The General Electric concept of all employees working together on the same team is distinctly different from the "group effort" approach to work. "Group responsibility and group decision-making imply a fallaciously comforting anonymity," says one internal paper, "making it possible for each individual in the group to avoid personal responsibility for results."[52] The company doctrine reflects the belief that no one person is then really accountable for the action of the group, and the alleged desirability of unanimity of action of a committee more often than not results in a course of action most secure, least risky, least courageous, perhaps with the highest probability of success but with limited results.[53]

Ray Brown notes that managers like decision-making committees. "They will use 'group decide' as an administrative fox hole in which to hide. Fearful of the administrative dark, they venture out only in the company of a committee."[54] Later, he pointed out that committees "become an escape mechanism for those administrators who can't take the organizational heat and who resort to presiding in order to avoid the personal responsibility of deciding."[55] The theory that individuals desire the comfortable anonymity of group action is, of course, counter to the belief that each individual wants to assume sole responsibility for his own actions and thus make the greatest possible contribution to the objectives of the component and the business enterprise.

This concept does not rule out the use of meetings and conferences for informative or stimulative purposes. There are committees in General Electric, such as safety committees, salary committees, and so forth, but these committees are for the purpose of determining or recommending what policy should be. They are not decision-making committees. One man is always responsible for the attainment of outcome. If seven people are on an advisory committee, only one man—whether he is a member of that committee or not—and only that one man is held 100 percent accountable for the decision that is made. Cordiner felt that advisory committees must get the best minds that can be utilized on any particular subject, but only one man can make the decision. That is good business. Thus, the popularity of "brain-storming" sessions is well earned. Their value for idea generation has been proved in practice. But these "brain-storming" sessions should be considered for what they really are: group stimulation of individual efforts. One internal document said that these committees "can often be the catalyst helping create ideas more quickly than by individual thinking in isolation."[56]

Assistant and Assistant To

Lieutenant Colonel Lyndall Urwick, who is an advocate of the "assistant to" position, wrote:

It is extremely difficult to make "assistant to" positions work smoothly in business. This is not because they are unnecessary: many Chief Executives are grossly overworked. And their undertakings suffer in consequence. But, they [the superiors] can't get their immediate subordinates to accept communications from an "Assistant to," because such communications appear to infringe the unofficial status symbolism of the undertaking—a Captain is ordering a Colonel about (to use a military parallel).[57]

Although Urwick admits business has had some difficulty with the "assistant to" position, he nevertheless advocates its use. Urwick and Dale correctly note that "assistant to" is normally inferior in status to his chief's immediate subordinates, has no authority of his own, issues instructions only as a representative of his chief's authority, and cannot replace his chief in his absence.[58]

Theoretically, without responsibility or authority, "assistant to" positions are found in many business and military organizations. In the military, the "assistant to's" function is primarily to convey the decisions and orders of his chief and he is known as a general staff officer. Urwick says, "An 'assistant to' position involves an officer of junior status [rank] sending instructions to his superiors in status."[59] He goes on:

In Armies everyone accepts the Fiction that they are his superior's orders, even when the recipients are perfectly well aware that his superior has never seen them. That is because status is defined by rank. And it is so unthinkable that an officer of inferior status should be issuing orders to an officer of superior status, say a Captain issuing orders to a Colonel, that Colonels at a lower echelon accept that a Staff Officer is merely acting as a Post Officer (or a Secretary) to his General.
Personally, I am convinced that a great deal of the personal friction which occurs in civil establishments can be traced to the fact that they have not yet "grown up" in this particular. Men are concerned about status. . . . They build unofficial status symbols. Any arrangement which appears to ignore or run counter to this symbolism excites resentment and retaliation.[60]

Urwick does believe that the "assistant to" should be given a dignified status. "Nothing deteriorates the morale of an assistant to more than becoming known as a bronze key to the president's toilet," has been attributed to Urwick, although he denies making the statement.[61]

There were a number of reasons why General Electric used "Assistant" or "Assistant to" positions before 1953.

1. To relieve excessive load on the Boss.
2. To train the man in broader duties.
3. To give the man a special title or status.
4. To give the able man more work to do and to challenge his ability.
5. To give authority to check others in detail.
6. To provide an "understudy" for the Boss.
7. To break in a successor to take over the Manager's job.[62]

Each of the above reasons for using an "assistant" was easily ruled out under the new philosophy. An overloaded boss must learn to delegate. A man can gain experience and broaden his duties by the use of staff meetings, proper job placement, and rotation. A man can be rewarded by higher pay and a more challenging job, with an appropriate title. A man can get a bigger and more responsible job within the company's basic organization structure through a specialist job or a managerial job of stature commensurate with his full ability. Men needing detailed checking should be replaced with competent performers who won't need to be so checked or audited; it's not sound economics to pay twice for getting work done right once. The use of a "title" instead of a more specific designation of work makes job titles unclear and adds to organizational confusion. In addition, a man has more pride as a manager than an "assistant" to someone else. When breaking in a successor to take over a manager's job it is sound business to allow a man to act as an "assistant" only for a limited period when the actual succession is imminent and the "assistant" must really get into all the phases of the boss's job. This type of short-term "assistant" position must not be refilled when the "assistant" moves into the boss's chair. Even this latter argument was not acceptable in General Electric: the successor was appointed immediately, and the incumbent was removed and used as a consultant, when necessary. This maintained clear relationships and pinpointed responsibility.

During the early years of formulating the philosophy of management at General Electric, a number of management practices were discovered that did not fit in with the emerging philosophy. As Smiddy was developing the principles of delegation (Figure 3-5), it became clear that these principles ran counter to some of the structure used by the enterprise. "Assistant" and "Assistant to" positions were counter to the developing philosophy for two major reasons: first, it was felt that these positions were not the best way to get work done under the principles of delegation and of organization structuring which had developed; and second, there was a better organization structuring of positions for stimulating self-development of individuals.

The first major point in reference to the principles of delegation can be seen from reading Figure 3-5. A responsibility cannot be shared by two or more individuals (point 5). An individual has responsibility or he does not (point 11). If the assistant has responsibility for helping his manager by doing part of the work, then General Electric philosophy claims "he is simply being a clerk, a messenger, or 'leg man.' "[63] If, on the other hand, a manager truly delegates a piece of work to an "assistant," then that "assistant" is no different from any other subordinate reporting to the manager.

If a subordinate is not given specific work to do, for which he is accountable, then a man would take on some unknown responsibility and confusion would reign, as no one would know for what the subordinate is accountable. Also, other men reporting to the manager would not know the relationship between themselves and the "assistant." Thus, in the General Electric philosophy, assistants are believed to violate a number of sound principles of delegation: responsibility is not clearly defined; their commensurate accountability is unclear; assistants may add another level of management; other subordinates may be unable to identify the relationships and at times believe they have more than one boss.

The second general reason that these positions violate corporate philosophy is that the firm feels the position structure inhibits self-development of individuals. The following four points are used by General Electric to demonstrate this belief:

1. Men who are acting as errand boys for their managers may gather much information by observation; but they do not have the stimulating opportunities to "learn by doing" as far as making their own decisions are concerned, coupled with the sometimes painful mind—and judgment—sharpening experience of having to live personally with the results of those decisions.

2. Men who get in the habit of gathering information requested by their manager so that he can make better decisions, run the risk of also getting in the habit of letting him do the thinking as well as the deciding.

3. The best men will not let themselves get stuck for long in "assistant" positions, because they are not satisfied unless they are responsible and accountable for work which is uniquely their own.

4. Experience has shown that men develop their managerial abilities and their self-confidence and belief in themselves faster and more surely if they have complete personal responsibility and accountability for a particular piece of work, even, though it be small, than they do when they have some unknown and necessarily fractional part of their manager's larger responsibilities.[64]

General Electric had thousands of "assistants" in 1952. At that time, Harold Smiddy went to Ralph Cordiner and asked him if he would mind giving up his assistant.

Cordiner asked, "Well, Harold, what for?"

"Why do you need the position?" asked Smiddy.

"Well, I need an assistant. Good Lord, I'm out of New York many, many times, travel quite a bit and when I'm not around I got a lot of things that have to be taken care of right away. And I need a very capable assistant."

And Smiddy says, "Well, what important decisions do you permit him to make when you're out of town?"[65]

Cordiner at this time was preaching management by exception, so it was implied that decisions made by Cordiner could not have been made by the executive vice presidents. Cordiner's assistant was a knowledgeable, well-respected performer, and considered very bright. However, no one would have even entertained the thought that this assistant could have made decisions on issues which were above the capabilities of the executive vice presidents.

Cordiner answered Smiddy by saying, "I'm beginning to get your point. What you're telling me is that I need a male secretary, possibly."

"That's right. And that goes for the rest of the company, too," added Smiddy. "I don't understand why anyone needs an assistant."

Cordiner immediately decided to remove the assistant positions throughout the company's organization structure. At this time there were thousands of assistants; nearly every one of them was a very capable man and Smiddy thought these capable men were rotting on the vine. In fact, within a year after the discontinuation of these assistants jobs many of the incumbents had become section managers; some had become general managers of departments. Many were to rise to the executive level after a few years. These people had been given their titles of assistant because they had earned them, and they were capable individuals.

When Smiddy went to the Chairman of the Board, Philip Reed, to talk with him about his assistant, Reed said, "Yes, I was talking to Ralph about that. I don't know what to do with him. He's a very capable individual and one of the most knowledgeable persons in the company, but I can't see him as a manager, though. He's just a great thinker."

Smiddy appointed the man as a consultant and assigned him to many tricky research problems in management. He proved to be an extremely capable man and was quite happy in his new enviornment, where he could be on his own.

Smiddy felt that in many instances "assistant to" and "assistant" positions were fictitious. Such positions were brought into being because a superior wanted to reward someone who had been doing outstanding work, but didn't know how to give him a proper award other than making him an assistant manager or assistant to somebody; and in doing so, General Electric forgot that one of the greatest developers of people is to give them problems, team projects, responsibility, and high pay. Unfortunately, many of these assistants, while they received good money, did not receive extraordinary pay in any sense. Smiddy's philosophy always was, "Pay the man and pay him well."

Shortly after Smiddy's conversation with Cordiner, Cordiner announced that all people who became department managers, section managers, or consultants in the various services were going to get extremely high pay because they were now in heavy risk positions. If they made errors, they were going to be released from their positions, and no one was going to take care of them. Because they were in such vulnerable positions, Cordiner said, "I'm going to pay you well and if you don't measure up I'm not going to worry about it. I'll get someone else who can do the job." So it was with that kind of offer that these individuals came into Services and others became general managers.

Frequently when you have five or six people reporting to a man, and you elevate one of them to an assistant spot, essentially what you have done is eliminate competition among those who remain, because you have appointed the man who ultimately will take over. The heir apparent to the throne has been selected, thereby killing initiative in the pack that is left. Smiddy had always contended, though, that an assistant makes work, especially if he is working for a very capable manager. The capable manager will continue to make the decisions and will use this assistant as an errand boy, one who runs around getting information but never making decisions. He gets out of the *habit* of making decisions. In time he loses his effectiveness, so that if after several years as an assistant he goes out into the real world of decision-making, he is incapable of making decisions.

General Electric found that when a man became an assistant and he was working under a capable department manager whom he was being groomed to replace ultimately, he frequently hired a secretary, because this was a status symbol and he had to have one for his own image. Since the department manager was strong and capable there was insufficient work for the assistant. To give him something to do, he initiated a project of his own. Once the project got going, the assistant would decide that what he needed was some young people to get information and analyze it. He wasn't going to do the whole project by himself. Besides, you should always delegate to the lowest level of competency. He would hire one, then two, while he was thinking of a new project. In time, maybe five years, he might have a staff of as many as fifteen or twenty people. When he took over the general manager's job or the manager to whom he reported, he would continue the assistant position on the grounds that if his predecessor needed an assistant, he certainly did, too. "It was self-perpetuating," says Greenwood, "so that when General Electric got rid of about ten thousand assistants, whatever the number might have been, they actually got rid of maybe fifty thousand or sixty thousand jobs. (Much of this work was reorganized into other parts of the structure.) That was the ultimate impact in streamlining the company."

At first the argument, of course, was "I'm working overtime now: I do need an assistant." It is true that people at times have a lot of work to do, and it is true that they sometimes get themselves somebody whom they call an assistant to take part of the load off their own back, but the key to it is always better organization. Some men would work eighty hours a week whether they had one assistant or forty. "In a study that was conducted by Management Consultation and other Services," says William Greenwood, "it was pretty well proved that people who hired assistants in the past on the basis of being overworked themselves found that the assistants never cured that situation. These men, for the most part, continued to work the same number of hours as they did before because some people would make eighty hours' work out of boiling water." As Parkinson notes, "An official wants to multiply subordinates, not rivals."[66]

One of the death-dealing considerations for the assistant position is that an assistant usually is one who speaks for the boss; or at least it is assumed he is. Those who have worked for managers who had assistants were always in a bind, especially when they were given conflicting orders, and this was not rare. William Greenwood comments:

Conflicting orders were a way of life and I received more than my share, especially while I was in the financial area. This did not surprise me because it was a well-known fact that usually the Assistant tried to usurp power. He tried to convey power that he did not have; he tried to be very important. And since he had really no job, no real job with any authority, in order to maintain his own status, his own respectability, he became a pompous ass very, very frequently, and usually it occurred immediately following his appointment. The two went hand in hand.

Urwick contends that Smiddy and General Electric really deplored the "assistant to" concept, not for the above reasons, but because they simply couldn't make the concept work. He says,

GE put up the old Accountants' argument. Because status is ill-defined in civil life, having an "Assistant to" became a status symbol in GE. So, all kinds of people started appointing "Assistants to," not because they needed them but because having "Assistant to" in a box below them on the organization chart was as good as adding a crown to their two stars. It gave them a push up in their status symbolism. That was expensive. So, the accounting viewpoint stepped in and it was classified as "unnecessary."[67]

Whatever the case, the titles and positions of "assistant" and "assistant to" are not presently acceptable to General Electric organization theory. Ralph Cordiner said, in reference to "assistants to" and "administrative assistants":

It is our firm belief that such titles or positions create confusion as to responsibility, authority, and accountability, and tend to retard the growth of men and the Company. If a position is too big for one person and appears to require assistants, then the work should be divided up and reorganized into as many positions as are required to do the work efficiently. Each position in the Company should be able to "stand on its own," with a specifically defined area of responsibility, authority, and accountability.[68]

Conclusion

Large organizations can be managed not by a single brain, but through coordinated decisions made by many. Just how decisions are to be thus delegated and the resulting actions coordinated is the central question in organization design.[69]

So it is with the design of decentralization in the General Electric Company. Before 1951 General Electric was centralized in the common meaning of the word, with committees as the central means for coordination. After 1950 decentralization became the gospel and committees for decision-making were eliminated.

After his organization study, Cordiner felt that General Electric's basic problem was not its huge size, but rather the diversity of its products.[70] He once said, "General Electric may well be the most diversified company in the world."[71] Therefore, Cordiner decentralized or fragmented the company into product departments. Each department has relative independence in decisions. Although this plan, in theory, solved many day-to-day operating problems, the decentralization into product or operating departments could have created a coordination and long-range planning problem. The development of the Executive Office with the chief executive officer, group vice presidents, and services executives has filled the function of coordination and long-range planning. In terms of control, the executive management, above the operating department, has authority to review and appraise the performance of the operating departments.

Cordiner thought through the philosophy of the new organization over a period of several years, and had his management philosophy documented in book form long before completing his implementation program. Few large firms, even to this day, have attempted to think through and record their corporate philosophy. Paul Mills saw that, before the philosophy became organized, General Electric was moving dangerously toward "an organization without sense of common identity, without a recognition of common objectives, and without a sense of mutual responsibilities and purposes."[72] General Electric, or more specifically, Cordiner, wanted to organize the firm to find out where it was going, to give it common identity, common objectives, and a sense of mutual responsibilities and purpose.

The corporate philosophy is not fully developed. General Electric claims it is still doing "pure research" on management theory and practice. The philosophy thus far organized is a foundation on which the firm operates. The philosophy is a structure to give direction; it is not final, for it is still being tested and redefined. It has proved to be a successful philosophy in terms of the fact that the company has been highly profitable throughout the period in which the philosophy was developed and practiced. The point is that the firm has been actively thinking of the theory, for, as one distinguished writer said: "The man who says he has no time for theory is either using a theory someone else has developed, or even a theory someone else has discarded."[73] The central point is that each company should study its environment so as to evolve a philosophy and structure that is appropriate for each individual company.

The decentralization philosophy was not adopted capriciously, but only after deep debate, long consideration, and extensive research. It was the Special Planning Committee inside General Electric that concluded in 1943 that the firm was going to grow very large after the war, and that a complete reorientation of thinking regarding the organization, the structure, and the philosophy of the company was necessary. In 1945 Cordiner, with President Wilson's endorsement, concluded that it was vital that General Electric develop and then adopt a philosophy of decentralization which embraced not only physical decentralization, but also decentralization of authority, responsibility, and decision-making. "In addition," notes Smiddy, "it was necessary to develop a top physical structure within the Company's organization which would preserve the Company as a corporate entity, assure its future progress and growth in established businesses, and enable it to move forward into new areas of technological, economic, and sociological advancement."[74] The philosophy may seem somewhat obscure, but the result has been to put the responsibility for operational decision-making into the hands of hundreds of managers in the third and fourth level of management, instead of in the hands of a few top executives.

4 Controlling Decentralization

GE began a study in late 1951, not yet completed,[1] on how to measure the work performed by departments, divisions, and individuals. This "Measurements Project," as it is called, is the key to understanding the philosophy behind the control function of the firm. This chapter describes the company's goal setting or budgeting and measuring, and also includes the conclusions thus far drawn.

Concluding the chapter is a discussion on budgeting and planning. Before decentralization (1951), planning and budgeting were top-echelon operations, and decisions made at this level were then handed down to subsequent levels until they reached the foreman level. Before decentralization managers below the vice-president level were given their budgets. Such decisions were handed down, level by level. Decentralization, in philosophy, changed this to what is called "bottoms-up" budgeting.

Measurements

Ralph Cordiner underscored the importance of measurements when he defined the concept of professional management as "the task of administration of a business enterprise through the leadership of its personnel to achieve its objectives by planning, organizing, measuring, and integrating its human and material resources."[2] In the latter part of 1951, he raised a question with the Advisory Committee as to whether the measurements area was not of sufficient importance to the company's future to warrant a comprehensive study. In early 1952, Management Consultation Services Division was assigned the responsibility for investigating measurements. In May 1952, Vice President Harold F. Smiddy appointed Fred J. Borch, and subsequently in late 1952 Robert W. Lewis, to develop the intensive research of this essential area. Until early 1953, the Measurements Project was a cooperative effort of the Management Consultation Services Division and the Accounting Services Division. On May 1, 1953, when Fred Borch returned to the Lamp Division, the Accounting Services Division took responsibility for the project.[3]

The objectives of the Measurements Project were five in number:

1. To find methods to measure the performance of the organizational components, not of individuals.
2. To find common indexes of performance but not to develop common

59

standards; i.e., rate of return on investment is a common index, but the standard in terms of what percent is wanted as a return on investment is not a concern of the project.

3. To realize that the measurements are designed for supplementing, not supplanting, judgment.

4. To find measurements which can be used both for current results and future projections.

5. To keep measurements at a minimum for each level of the organization.[4]

This Measurements Project is the key to understanding the control function within the firm. Out of this project came most of the quantitative control mechanisms and some of the qualitative controls used today. Therefore, a deeper study of the project appears warranted.

The project was divided into three subprojects:

1. Operational measurements, of which there are eight, identified as key result areas.

2. Functional measurements—engineering, manufacturing, marketing, finance, employee and plant community relations, and legal.

3. Measurements of the work of managing—planning, organizing, integrating, and measuring [General Electric's definition of the work of a manager].

In developing operational measurements, a search was attempted of specific areas for which measurements should be designed. When an area was being tentatively investigated to see if it was vital to the organization, the following test question was applied: "Will continued failure in this area prevent the attainment of management's responsibility for advancing General Electric as a leader in a strong, competitive economy, even though results in all other key result areas are good?"[5]

Within operational measurements, the project leaders concluded that there were eight areas of such vital importance to the welfare of the company as to merit the development of measures for each of them. The eight key result areas as developed by Fred Borch, and subsequently reconfirmed by Lewis, are listed below, along with Peter Drucker's eight areas in which objectives of performance and results have to be set. The similarity of the lists is striking, but not so striking when it is realized that Drucker was, during the early fifties, an outside consultant assisting General Electric in the Measurements Project, and was therefore in close contact with Vice President Harold F. Smiddy, head of Management Consultation Services, Fred Borch, and Robert Lewis, as head of the Measurements Project.

General Electric's Key Result Areas	Drucker's Major Objective Areas
1. Profitability	1. Profitability
2. Market Position	2. Market Standing
3. Productivity	3. Productivity

General Electric's Key Result Areas	*Drucker's Major Objective Areas*
4. Product Leadership	4. Innovation
5. Personnel Development	5. Manager Performance and Development
6. Employee Attitudes	6. Worker Performance and Attitude
7. Public Responsibility	7. Public Responsibility
8. Balance Between Short-Range and Long-Range Goals[6]	8. Physical and Financial Resources[7]

Profitability

Profitability is considered by many, especially economists and accountants, as well as the less sophisticated public, as the ultimate measurement of business performance in our competitive free economy. Drucker sees two other purposes for profits: not only are they the ultimate test of the performance of a business, but also "the risk premium" which covers the costs of staying in business and market risk.[8] Third, profits make possible the funds for expansion and research—for self-financing out of retained earnings or for providing inducement for new outside capital.[9] He goes on to note, correctly, that

none of these three functions of profit has anything to do with the economist's maximization of profit. All these three are indeed "minimum" concepts—the minimum of profit needed for the survival and prosperity of the enterprise. A profitability objective, therefore, measures not the maximum profit the business can produce, but the minimum it must produce.[10]

Thus, profitability has value as one of the many measurements of business performance; value is derived as long as we understand what profitability is measuring and what it is not. Used as the *only* measure of business performance, profitability will distort.

In any business enterprise, profits are produced by the combination of capital and work. There has been a tendency to consider profits in relation only to the capital invested; hence, return on invested capital has been a time-honored business measurement of performance. A high rate of profit in terms of invested capital is a sure way of attracting new outside capital. However, any perceptive manager realizes that the efforts of the organization, that is, the work performed, in combination with the invested capital produces profits. Since an executive manager has the responsibility to change the relationships and amounts of both, he is interested in measuring the results of his action. In complex large organizations with numerous and diverse product lines, the manager must weigh not only the physical resources utilization among the various businesses or product lines, but also the human resources and how they should be utilized.

The stockholder's point of view is that of maximum profits in relation to his investment. The shareholder's only contribution is his investment; therefore, it is only natural that he measure the profits of the business in terms of earnings in relation to it.

General Electric sets up a profitability index in answer to the question, "What profitability index gives a properly weighted consideration to both capital and work, as seen by the shareowner and executive manager?"[11]

From the viewpoint of the executive manager and shareowner, General Electric developed indexes of profitability under the criterion that profitability measurement must recognize the contributions of both capital and work. The Measurements Project, after studying the problem, developed four criteria which the firm has followed since 1954:

1. Does the index recognize that capital investment has contributed to the profits?
2. Does the index recognize that the work performed by the business has contributed to the profits?
3. Does the index recognize the corporate "facts of life"?
4. Most important, will the use of the index work to guide decisions in the company's best interest?[12]

The third and fourth criteria point out that the measurement index must possess the following characteristics:

It should be realistic.
It should be understandable.
It should have the confidence of operating management.
It should be consistent with the organizational philosophy.[13]

There are a number of methods of computing a figure called "profit." Such terms and relations as controllable profits, incremental profits, real economic earnings, and book profits as recorded under conventional accounting procedures are all some type of "profit" figure. General Electric concluded that the "book profit" concept was and still is most appropriate for measuring the performance of its business.

It is easy to understand why the controllable profits and incremental profits were discarded as an overall measure of the performance of the business or product line. Under these two concepts only the "controllable" or "variable" costs are deducted from revenue to arrive at profit, which is not realistic in terms of the third criterion, that the corporate "facts of life" must be considered. A business must be held responsible for the "noncontrollable" or "fixed costs" as well.

Real economic earnings—which are, simply, book profits adjusted to a replacement cost basis—were discarded as a proper measure of business success for two reasons. First, the theory of replacement cost is unreal, in that it is unlikely that existing facilities will be replaced in kind; and second, there is no practical method of computing replacement cost values on which there is general agreement as to its validity. Therefore, the economic earning concept would not be consistent with the "facts of life" and would not have the confidence of the operating managers.

It must be remembered—and presumably General Electric understands—that operating managers will inevitably try to make profit decisions that will improve their results in terms of the profits measurement selected. That is to say, if the measurement index is "the ratio of profits to X," then the manager will strive to make this index look good. While the "ratio of profits to Y" is also important to the business, it too should be incorporated as an index by which results are to be measured. This must be the thinking of General Electric, as more than one index is used as a gauge. General Electric uses book profits as the general type of index for internal control of product lines in the operating units. It has three indexes of book profits: residual dollar profit; percent residual dollar; and profit to contributed value.

To understand how these indexes are used as control mechanisms and the value which can be or is attributed to them, a look at the conventional book-profit indexes is of value. In looking at conventional indexes of profitability for strengths and weaknesses, profitability should also be evaluated in terms of the four criteria which the firm set up.[14]

The following measurements of profitability are used by some firms:

Total dollars of profit
Percent profit to sales
Rate of return on investment (ROI)
Percent profit to contributed value
Percent profit to value added
Percent profit to total employee costs
Percent profit to professional employee costs.

Each of these methods to measure profits and to control the work of product executive managers has merit; yet there is weakness in each which must be understood if proper evaluation and measurement interpretation are to be expected.

Total dollars of profit as a sound control measure is usually dismissed by accounting texts. It can be dismissed because it does not fulfill two of the four criteria: it does not recognize capital investment, nor does it distinguish between the work of the business itself and that of its suppliers. Yet it is important. Dividends are paid out of profit dollars. As Robert Lewis aptly puts it,

"Dividends are paid from profit dollars—not ratios—and for complete concentration on maximizing profits, there is no better index than Total Dollars of Profits."[15]

Percent profit to sales is a popular accounting favorite, yet it also fails to recognize capital investment. This is important, because if percent profit to sales is used as the sale index, it would encourage the business to improve its percent to sales by using depreciation as the only determinant in deciding investments in plant and equipment. It would encourage the overlooking of inventory and other working capital. By the second criterion, the ratio does not distinguish between the work of the business and its suppliers, because it measures profit in relation to the market value of the combined efforts of the vendors and the business. Percent profit to sales could dampen the incentive for the more profitable business to grow. A department with a profit ratio of 7 percent to sales will add new products on which it can make 8 percent, while a department with a ratio of 12 percent will tend to turn down products on which it expects to make 8 percent. Thus, the total company might tend to expand in the least profitable direction, because each department has a different yardstick or goal.

The most widely used index of profitability is the rate of return on investment (ROI). ROI is especially important as a measuring and control device because it relates profits to the capital invested in the business, and therefore gives an accounting of the effect of managerial decisions to the shareholder's interests. ROI does reflect the contribution of capital; that is its design. On point 2, however, it muddles the contribution of the firm with its suppliers. Also, it may force concentration on short-term profit returns at the expense of the long run. ROI has the effect of averaging down the overall company rate of return, just as the percent profit to sales does.

The ROI index is subject to the criticism that each profit center or division tends to regard its own current rate of return as the criterion against which to measure investment decisions, with the result that a decentralized firm will have as many different criteria as there are profit centers. John Dearden emphasizes this point in one of his attacks on the ROI in the *Harvard Business Review:*

In a decentralized company, there may be wide variations in the rate of return expected from the different divisions. It is not uncommon, for example, to find divisional rates of return on investment varying from zero (or even a negative rate) to as much as 30% after taxes. This situation creates a problem because the division with the 30% profit objective will be worse off for undertaking any capital project that earns less than 30%, while any return at all on a project will benefit the division with the zero profit objective.[16]

This means that the possibility exists that a high-return division may well turn down investments on which a greater return could be realized than on other investments being added at the same time by a low-return division. General Electric feels that a capital charge concept will overcome this problem found in the ROI by the mere fact that all department profit centers will evaluate decisions against the relatively simple criterion of whether or not the result of decisions will be to increase dollar profit beyond an amount needed to cover the capital damage. This is called "residual dollar profit."

Residual profit has the advantage of greater sensitivity in that it declines more slowly, proportionately, than does the ROI.

The measurements team researched each operating component (division) for the years 1951 through budget 1954, comparing results in terms of the proposed indexes under the firm's conventional indexes (i.e., percent net income to sales, return on investment, residual dollars, profit and percent residual profit to contributed value). The comparison showed that in the majority of instances residual dollar profit (RDP) and rate of return (ROI) reacted in the same manner—that is, when ROI increased, RDP increased, and when ROI decreased, RDP decreased. But the survey found over twenty instances in which the indexes conflicted—ROI decreased while RDP increased. It was felt, from evaluating the conflicts found, that RDP was an index showing a better indication of profitability than ROI, and it would encourage growth and expansion.[17]

The last four measures of profitability—percent profit to contributed value, percent profit to value added, percent profit to total employee costs, and percent profit to professional employee costs—all have major drawbacks. The percent profit to any one of the selected bases tends to regard depreciation as almost a sole determinant for the decision to invest in plant and equipment. It overlooks the tie-up of capital in inventories, plant and equipment, and receivables. All four fail to meet the fourth criterion—guidance in operating decisions. General Electric says:

[An] area of weakness for all these indices is the undesirable effect that any "measurement by ratio" tends to have on growth and balance. . . . Briefly, we feel that if a "ratio" measure is the sole criterion of profitability, decisions will be made by each business in terms of the effect that the decision will have on the particular business' current ratio without consideration of the dollar profits involved. The business with a high percent profit to contributed value, for example, would tend to turn down proposals which yield a lower profit ratio than that currently earned even though the lower ratio might be higher than the company-wide average.[18]

After an exhaustive research on possible indexes of profitability, the measurements team developed two indexes that are basically outgrowths of several of the indexes mentioned above. The project team recommended the use on a company wide basis of:

1. Residual dollar profit as a primary index
2. Percent residual dollar
3. Profit to contributed value as secondary index.

These were recommendations, as the project was a Services Division Study, and therefore could be used only as a suggestion to the line or operations divisions. Also, with a true decentralization philosophy, the executive group felt that operations must have the final say on how they should be measured. Maurice Mayo, Vice President and Comptroller, claims that even today there are no uniform measuring devices and that the only reason for having some accounts kept in uniformity is for tax purposes.[19]

Examination of these measurements is helpful in order to understand how they act as control devices. Residual dollar profit is an index which represents the net book profit minus a capital charge.[20] That is, federal taxes shall be deducted from income to give net book value.

The capital charge will be expressed as a percent of each department's average net investment, and it is recommended that it represent *a minimum acceptable return after taxes.* It is desirable that the charge be set as closely as possible to the point at which discontinuance of the business will be considered. The implication will be that a business that is not returning the capital charge and has no prospect of doing so over a reasonable period of time is an unsatisfactory one from the viewpoint of executive management and the shareowner, and therefore consideration should be given to its discontinuance.[21]

The secondary index, percent residual dollar profit to contributed value, is a ratio with half of the ratio centered on contributed value. Again, contributed value is simply the difference between sales revenue and the aggregate cost of materials and parts ("direct material") purchased from others for incorporation in the finished product for resale. The subtracting out of the cost of purchased raw materials and parts is sensible according to the theory of "value added in manufacturing" accounting.[22] Drucker wrote on this subject:

The single major cost category that is usually clearly identifiable with respect to a specific product is irrelevant to the revenue contribution and to the share of the cost burden. This is the cost for purchased raw materials and parts. A simple example—taken from a company making small electrical household appliances such as toasters, coffee makers, and flat irons—will illustrate this:

Purchased materials and parts account for sixty percent of the manufacturer's price in the case of product A, for thirty percent in the case of product B. Both sell the same volume. Profit margin is ten percent of manufacturer's price for both products. Both therefore are believed to do equally well. But actually the manufacturer makes one dollar in profits for any three dollars worth of his own resources and efforts invested in product A; he has to spend six dollars worth of his own resources and efforts to make one dollar on product B. If both products had a ready market for a larger output at the same price, though the manufacturer had resources to expand only one, he would get twice as much additional output by putting his resources into product A rather than into product B. An additional unit of product A requires only thirty dollars worth of resources against a requirement of sixty dollars for product B. He would therefore get twice as much profit through expanding product A rather than product B.[23]

The question might and should arise, do the indexes meet the four criteria as set out by the company? The fact is that no one index meets the criteria, but the double-index approach does.

The first criterion is the recognition of capital investment, which is met by the residual dollar profit index, to use General Electric terminology, or the more common name of "value added" approach. As was previously stated, most indexes tend to encourage decisions which consider only operating costs, and to overlook the tie-up of capital in inventories and other assets. Using a fixed minimum acceptable capital charge overcomes this.

The second criterion, recognizing the work of the business, is also satisfied by the two indexes. The residual dollar profit index alone does not fully recognize the work of the business. Even when the percent residual dollar profit to contributed value is used, it is not a full measure of performance. General Electric feels, "It is the best available measure of the value placed by the marketplace on the combined human and machine effort expended by the business."[24]

Recognition of the corporate facts of life is the third criterion, and General Electric's subjective judgment is that the two indexes show just that and that they will have the confidence of operation managers. Lewis reports, "In our opinion the concepts which we are recommending approximate, as closely as is practicable, what the facts would be if each business were a separate corporate entity."[25]

The last criterion, a guide to making decisions in the company's best interests, is met according to the firm, although some outside accountants might take issue with this.

The residual dollars profit index encourages concentration on improving the dollar profit rather than the improvement of ratios. "Under the proposed index," claims the Measurements Project team, "management will be encouraged to make decisions which will improve *dollar* profit rather than the ratio to selected base."[26]

Residual dollar profit index has the inherent drawback that many managers may believe that the attainment of the percent of net investment at which the capital charge is fixed represents a satisfactory performance. To avoid this, the measurements team suggests that it should be made clear that:

1. The capital charge is a minimum acceptable return.
2. Any business [profit center] which cannot see its way clear to meet this "subsistence level" of return will be carefully studied as to whether we should continue in that business.
3. The *standard* of profit performance will be expressed as Dollar Residual Profit; i.e., the dollars of profit *above* the capital charge.[27]

With establishment of the concept of residual dollar profit and the secondary index—percent residual dollar profit to contributed value—General Electric next faced the problem of setting standards. The method of measurement is only half of the first step of control. Once the method is determined, the problem of what is considered par for the course must be faced. Setting standards is at least as difficult as developing the measurement itself. Standards are judgments—subjective goals based on forecasts. Standards are tied to budgets. Companies do not or should not start with a rate of return and work back. They start with a forecast of what can be expected in sales and what, therefore, is needed for sales and inventory. Then the cost is evaluated. This is an oversimplication of budget preparation, but the point is that ultimately all the planning is converted into dollars and a standard of performance is produced by examining the inputs and outputs of each item contributing to the end result. Lewis writes, "And in the final analysis you must exercise judgment as to what is the optimum you can expect under the particular set of conditions with which you are faced."[28] The particular standards as used today are of no importance to this study, even if they could be published. The particular index standards are not important; only how they are developed and used is of significance.

The project report emphasized that the proposed indexes did not overcome one important weakness. A weakness of all known indexes is that they help develop a desire to realize immediate profits at the expense of future profits. For as many years as any person interviewed can remember, when preparing annual budgets, General Electric executives have forecast for at least five years. Of course, there may be slight resemblance between actual results for 1979 and a budget for 1979 prepared in 1974 because of environmental changes. But management must subjectively, at least, not let the standards pressure them toward present profits at the expense of the future. The discussion on this subject will be expanded when we look at key result area No. 8, "Balance Between Short-Range and Long-Range Goals."

Market Position

The second area of control for operating managers is in the measurement of market position. Market position measurements reflect the total business. It is a measurement of "the acceptance of a company's products and services by the market and thus reflects the value of the company's products, its distributing and promotional policies, and its technological contributions."[29] Therefore, measurement of market position is essential in order to receive indications of progress being made toward the attainment of growth and leadership, which are two of the company's objectives.

Although the marketing function may have a predominant interest in the measurement of market position, the results achieved are dependent upon the contributions of all the functions. Marketing must be properly understood as the only revenue producer of the operational functions; the others are all cost centers.

Management's first responsibility is for the survival of the enterprise. It is having the right product, at the right price, at the right place, at the right time, with a public having this knowledge, which ensures the survival of the firm. Which means that the final focus for business activity has to be the end customers. This is a well-recognized marketing concept that is described as "a way of managing a business so that each critical business decision is made with a full and prior knowledge of the impact of that decision on the customer."[30]

In the course of testimony before a congressional subcommittee in 1949, the president of one of our great American companies said: "It is the customer, and the customer alone, who casts the vote. . . . The regulations laid down by the consuming public are far more potent and far less flexible than any code of law, merely through the exercise of the natural forces of trade."[31]

The object of measuring the market position is to compare a product's actual sales with the opportunity available to that product for making sales. It is a partial control device helping to measure the effectiveness of the management. "The purpose of a business is to create a customer," Drucker has pointed out on a number of occasions.[32] The firm sees the creation of a customer as selling a product. The customer sees the other side of the coin; he sees his buying as satisfying a need. Therefore, a firm cannot properly conceive its market in terms of products, but it must define the market according to customers' wants and needs.

Drucker demonstrates that market standing must be measured against the market potential.[33] The measurements team reflects Drucker's belief by recommending that the total market available to a product be the basis for measurement. The measurements team recommended that the total available market be segregated into two major classifications, which they designed as served markets and unserved markets.[34] Markets are defined in terms of customer wants or in terms of uses to which the customer puts the products. This is the most intelligent method of defining markets—in terms of customers, rather than in terms of production. As Drucker notes:

To be able to set market-standing objectives, a business must first find out what its market is—who the customer is, where he is, what he buys, what he considers value, what his unsatisfied wants are. On the basis of this study the enterprise must analyze its products or services according to "lines"; that is, according to the wants of the customers they satisfy.

All electric condensers may look the same, be the same technically and come off the same production line. Market-wide, condensers for new radios may, however, be an entirely different line from condensers for radio repair and replacements and both again quite different from the physically indistinguishable condensers that go into telephones.[35]

Measuring market position is used as a control to see if the product, through management decision, is in the right market and is satisfying the right customer wants. Of course, the long-term objective of the use of measuring market position is to see to it that management has chosen to serve the more rapidly growing markets.

To be able to measure market standing and to set market-standing objectives, one must first determine what constitutes the market. A market must be defined in terms of a customer want—that is, the use to which a product is or may realistically be put by a customer. Competition within each market must be defined in terms of the substitutability of the products available to satisfy that want, as viewed by the customer. This definition of the market does not go as far as Drucker implies it should go. He shows how a Cadillac is mainly bought for prestige satisfaction, and that Cadillac competes for the customer's money with mink coats, jewelry, vacations, and other prestige satisfiers.[36] Nonetheless, General Electric has recognized what many firms have missed, that the market must be measured from the customer's point of view, from the use to which the product is put.

Leading from the customer viewpoint, General Electric recognized the total market concept; that is, taking the customer and his wants as a starting point. General Electric is usually credited with pioneering the modern marketing concept on which many marketing instructors have centered their courses. (And many have misrepresented this simple concept.)[37] All companies give at least lip service to the total market concept, but Drucker notes,

a good deal of what is called "marketing" today is at best organized, systematic selling in which the major jobs—from sales forecasting to warehousing and advertising—are brought together and coordinated. . . . But, its starting point is still our products, our customers, our technology. The starting point is still the inside.[38]

General Electric is organized by product departments; therefore, in that company's case, the

Total Market consists of those customers' wants that can be satisfied by products within *the assigned scope of the department*, whether or not the department is presently marketing products designed to answer those wants.[39]

Further breakdown of total market is made by use of served markets and unserved markets. Served markets represent customer wants which a department is striving to serve, and unserved markets are "those the department *can* serve under its assigned product scope but does not."[40]

An illustration of served and unserved markets appropriate to General Electric can be found in the lighting equipment business, or "lamp business," in company jargon. The department is permitted to sell both street-lighting and searchlight fixtures. It is obvious that the customer wants of the two are different and represent at least two distinct markets, although the production skill may be exactly the same. If the department decides to sell only street-lighting fixtures, that is its served market; then its potential searchlight-fixtures customers constitute its unserved market.

The department may elect to sell only one size of street-lighting fixtures, while other manufacturers are marketing models in several sizes. The unserved market would include sales not made to customers who buy sizes not produced by the firm.

There is a strong reason for a firm to measure its unserved markets, for it is another measure of management decisions. Management made the decision to cater to certain wants and not to others. Sometimes the decision by management to avoid a market is by default, rather than explicit. In either case, the effect of (or lack of) the decision must be ascertained. For this reason, both served and unserved markets—that is, retained and foregone markets—must be measured.

General Electric employs a third measure of marketing: the industry market, really a subclassification of served and unserved markets. This particular measurement is weak, and if it gains dominant position as a measurement stick it will hide the true customers from the firm. Industry market is oriented to a specific type or family of products, rather than to customer wants, and it includes, as competitive products, only those which are essentially the same as General Electric's. The company says:

In many of the markets in which our departments may participate, the products of more than one industry compete to satisfy the customer wants which that market represents. Because of the fact that in some of these instances it is unlikely that we would engage in the marketing of non-electrical products, it is imperative that we be constantly alert to the relative status of electrical and non-electrical products in the market place [i.e., stoves and refrigerators both are sold in electric and gas models].[41]

This measurement is most irrelevant as a device to measure the effectiveness of managerial decisions. Industry market is measuring the answer to the wrong questions. It is worried about the question, "Where is *our* market?" When the proper question is, "Where is *the* market?" Once a firm allows itself to believe that its products are fulfilling customer wants by thinking that its particular industry has tied up the wants, then it may be rudely awakened someday to find another industry has "stolen" the market. This is reminiscent of the waxed-paper industry, which found that the aluminum and plastic industries had found a way to satisfy the same customer wants.

From the above understanding of market position, the measurement team recommended two measurements for this key area: measurements of the department's position, and measurements of respective positions of the industry and served markets in which the department is performing.[42]

The primary yardstick is ratio of department's sales to served market sales.

This particular measure is an attempt to measure market position. Thus, products sold by manufacturers in other industries are often found to be competitors. Because of this somewhat broader concept of market for General Electric "businesses," most product lines found that their percent of share of market was lower than it was under the older, narrower, and more traditional concept of the market. GE's wider base definition of "market" in 1956 describes

a business [department] now showing a market share of 50 percent based on its present definition of market; they, using our definition, end up showing only 10 percent. . . . We have to re-educate ourselves as to what is good *standard* within the framework of the measurement index.[43]

Figure 4-1 gives the recommended market position measurements. It should also be noticed that in addition to the above mentioned measurements, the measurements study team also suggested the use of: (1) the estimated competitive rank within the served markets and industry market, and (2) the estimated share of these markets secured by leading competitors. Naturally, such measurements can only be educated guesses.

The measurements of market position only measure market position; they are not measures of the total marketing function. Taken singularly or totally, they are not measures of "marketivity"[a]—which must include marketing costs, or at least some estimate of marketing inputs, such as storage, moving, administrative costs, and so forth. General Electric does not consider marketing costs in any of the market measurements. Marketing costs are only part of the cost used in the figuring of profitability.

Measurement of the department's position
    Primary measure:
        Ratio of department's sales to served market sales
    Secondary measure:
        Ratio of department's sales to served industry market sales

Measurements of respective positions of the industry and served markets in which the department is participating
    Ratio of served industry market to served markets
    Ratio of served markets to total market

Supplemental measure
    Customer surveys to measure customer opinion of department's products and service performance

---

Figure 4-1. Market Position Measurements. Source: *Measurements Project Operational Measurement Key Result Area No. 2: Market Position* (Schenectady, N.Y.: General Electric Company, April 1956), p. 19.

---

[a]Marketivity is a term coined by Saul Silverstein, and is used for marketing as productivity is used for production.

The measurements team concludes:

We think that information of this kind is important to a manager not only in informing him on his position in the various markets but even more importantly in pointing up trends affecting the long-term interests of the department and, through the department, the company. A presentation of the actual sales of the various markets, coupled with a projection of potential sales, will be a valuable guide to advance planning and establishment of objectives.[44]

The company literature is always quick to point out that these measurements are used to help managers understand what is happening and, equally important, to help them evaluate their own managerial decisions. That is in line with their overall corporate philosophy of self-evaluation. A cornerstone of GE's decentralization philosophy is self-development—it allows for what General Electric has long preached, self-control. It also allows for a more quantifiable control from above.

Productivity

Productivity is the third key area of measurement for managers of operations. As an economic term, it is the relationship of output of goods and services to the resources, or inputs, consumed in their production. For the national economy, productivity is more frequently measured as the amount of output per unit of labor input. But labor is only one of the many factors contributing to output. The contributions of capital, or technology, and of knowledge are frequently overlooked in economic folklore as to their effects on productivity. Only since the pioneering work of Simon Kuznets have the factors of productivity other than labor received a great amount of consideration among the economists.[45] Discussing the economic advance of the last hundred years, Drucker claimed, "There has been no increase in the 'productivity' of labor."[46] There are very likely many who would disagree, but the fact is that almost all productivity increases can be attributed to application of advances in our knowledge. General Electric believes, "The bulk of the increases in productive efficiency comes from technological advances, creative innovation in products, and attendant progress in products, materials, facilities and methods, and in organization of the work."[47] It is the responsibility of a manager to plan, to organize, and to integrate these many different factors. It is the manager's responsibility to lead or motivate the employees to increase productivity. Productivity is a proper measure of a manager's success, since he is the coordinator of all the factors affecting it.

General Electric has not finished its research on how to measure productivity, but when the research is complete, the conclusions should add another yardstick by which managers can evaluate themselves and others. The preliminary investigation has brought up some worthwhile insights to productivity as a control device. The indexes of productivity for an economy as a whole are computed by the relation of GNP to total man hours worked. In developing an index of productivity for the firm, the figure of sales billed may be looked upon as the counterpart of GNP (output). Therefore, for a firm, productivity is the relationship between sales billed and employee man hours. General Electric has found other factors which may express productivity—output against input—and each has merits. A listing of the factors which may show productivity includes the following:

Output	Input
Sales billed	Man hours worked
Units sold	Payroll dollars
Value added	Equivalent man hours
Manufacturing cost	Floor space
Units produced	First cost of plant and equipment[48]

Other possible indexes have been developed. As a measure of output, sales billed is weak and could be misleading, as the firm may decide to buy materials in an advanced stage of fabrication or subcontract the manufacture of various component parts of a product. This would have no effect on sales billed, but man hours worked would be reduced and "productivity" would show a substantial improvement.

The Measurements Project team has been seeking to develop an index which would do two things:

(1) measure improvement in the productivity of our operations as distinguished from improvement contributed by our suppliers of materials, and (2) broaden the input base so as to recognize that capital as well as labor contributed to improvement in productivity.[49]

Hoping to recognize the value capital plays in conjunction with labor, General Electric began to study the possibility of using "value added" as a basis for determining productivity. "Value added" is defined by the firm as sales billed less the cost of goods and services purchased from other producers, whether incorporated in the end product or consumed in the operation of the business.[50] Value added is, in fact, what the company now uses as a basis for productivity. To avoid confusion, it should be mentioned that another possible basis is "contributed value." This is not used by GE. "Contributed value" is sales billed less the cost of goods or services actually incorporated in the end product only. On the input side of the ratio, GE has thought about using payroll dollars plus depreciation dollars as the input factor. Thus, productivity would be the ratio of value added to the sum of the two dollar figures. Both the input and output figures would be expressed in constant value to make it possible to see trends.

Product Leadership

The fourth type of measurement developed for the firm is product leadership. Again, this measurement reflects the performance of the business or product line as a whole, and should not be interpreted as a measurement of any one function. Product leadership is defined as

the ability of a business to lead its industry in originating or applying the most advanced scientific and technical knowledge in the engineering, manufacturing and marketing fields to the development of new products and to improvements in the quality or value of existing products.[51]

Two of the members of the team investigating General Electric's first attempt at measurement of performance in this qualitative area have been promoted to Vice President: Robert W. Lewis, Group Executive of the operational field, Power Transmission and Distribution; and John B. McKitterick, Vice President of the staff field, Planning Development. So this Measurements Project team was extremely high powered in terms of corporate administration positions held by the team members.

Product leadership is in the minds of the consumers and not what the manufacturer thinks, or should not be. Drucker notes, "There is no leadership if the market is not willing to recognize the claim."[52] This means in terms of what the customers are willing to pay. Product leadership is an economic term, not aesthetic, and is used as a measure of two or more products, by different firms. A monopolist cannot have product leadership because the consumer has no choice. The customer, by preferring one product to its competitor's, gives product leadership.

Therefore, product leadership should not be measured by the common test, "share of market." As often found, to get the largest share of the market, companies have to sacrifice profitability—compared to competitors. Thus, instead of getting paid to be the product leader, the firm is having to pay to get leadership. Drucker has found:

Some small manufacturers, each specializing in one or two special applications of low-horsepower electrical motors, have been doing proportionately better than General Electric or Westinghouse, whose dominant market share forces them to supply all kinds of motors to all customers and for all end users, and who therefore, of necessity, must be marginal or lose money on some lines.[53]

Drucker proposes that the following five questions be asked in analyzing products for their leadership position.

1. Is the product being bought in preference to other products on the market, or at least as eagerly?

2. Do we have to give anything to get the customer to buy?

3. Do we get paid for what we deliver to him as indicated by an at-least-average profit contribution?

4. Are we getting paid for what we think is the product distinction?

5. Or do we have a product with leadership position and with distinction without discerning it?[54]

The extent of product leadership, or lack of it, has a vital effect on the survival and growth of the firm. In a widely decentralized company the performance of one department in product leadership may have considerable influence in establishing customer acceptance of the products of other departments.

Because of the importance of this field, and because of the vitalness of this area to managerial decision-making, to properly evaluate a manager's performance it is necessary to develop a method of measuring product leadership.

Once product leadership has been determined, then the reasons this position was reached are of paramount importance. For instance, when a department's performance has been judged to be unsatisfactory, the appraisal should include why the department has lagged behind competitors. Did it fail to recognize market requirements? was it unable to solve engineering or manufacturing problems? or were there other causes?[55]

Appraisal of a department's existing products and the similar products of competitors will enable the department to determine how well its products satisfy customer wants, as compared with competitors' products. To continue as leaders, company products must be evaluated in terms of strengths—and weaknesses—which will allow the manager to develop offensive rather than defensive action.

The Electronics Business Development Study of 1955 pointed out the importance of being a leader in introducing new technical principles to the market.[56] The study pointed out that when General Electric made a late entry into the market with products which copied the technical principles of other firms, GE seldom achieved product leadership. The conclusion was that product market leadership resulted from leading or at least keeping pace in *introducing* new products to the market. This seems to emphasize that the firm cannot often afford to lag in introducing new products or it will lose leadership. Emphasis on being first or early in marketing products will not, it is hoped, encourage the premature marketing of new products or product improvement. Of course, the measurement team did point out that delay in entering a market may give rise to lost prestige, reduced volume, and less profits resulting from the time advantage given to competitors.

When evaluating the leadership of various products, a qualitative evaluation has to be used. But General Electric measures performance, which is a measure of past managerial decisions, by appraising the firm's existing products to determine:

1. How they compare with competitors' products and with General Electric standards.

2. The source of the research on which the products are based.

3. Whether the basic product and subsequent product improvements were first introduced by General Electric or by competition.[57]

In conjunction with the second point, Ted Quinn, long-time head of General Electric's lamp department, was able to say in 1953,

I know of no original product invention, not even electric shavers or heating pads, made by any of the giant laboratories of corporations, with the possible exception of the household garbage grinders, developed not by the Research Laboratory but by the engineering department of General Electric.... The record of giants is one of moving in, buying out, and absorbing the smaller creators.[58]

Oddly enough, Drucker was to write a decade later, "General Electric seems to have had little luck with the businesses it acquires."[59]

Each department must determine standards from the standpoint of the customer, for General Electric holds that the customer sets the standards. This view would prevent a product from looking superior on paper by being "overengineered" beyond the desires of the market. Standards must be set by sampling the market at regular intervals to ascertain what the customer wants in way of performance, features, and attractiveness in products, and also in terms of what the customer is willing to pay. The results of these surveys will help develop standards against each product which can be appraised to determine the "leading product."

It is easy to see that General Electric is developing a true control structure in this area. First, it has set objectives—to have leading products. Second, it has organized the particular measurements—performance, features, and attractiveness in the eyes of the consumers. Third, it has set standards—they are flexible and subjective, but they are standards.

Separate standards must be developed for each market because General Electric correctly defines products, not from the manufacturing needs, but from the customers' needs. A product doing well in one market may be weak in another. General Electric says,

Based on survey results ... and the informed judgment of the department management, weighted numerical values may be assigned to the various factors of performance, features and attractiveness (depending upon the relative importance of each in a particular market) to arrive at a product standard.[60]

For determining the overall rating for each product, the products should be evaluated from the standpoint of how they compare with the standards based on market requirements. Some evaluation can be expressed in numerical terms and some must be expressed subjectively. Qualitative measurements, when used correctly, can be as useful as quantitative measurements. The inability to express some inputs in absolute numerical terms should not detract from their use as evaluation aids. Although not an absolute figure, such a profile makes the process easier to control through management by exception.

Personnel Development[61]

Personnel development, Key Result Area No. 5, is another part of management that is future oriented. Edwin Flippo said that there are two general principles of executive development: all development is self-development; and an effective organizational climate must be established if the program is to be successful. As a corollary, he adds that it is a long-range process.[62] He then goes on to discuss coaching, job rotation, special courses, and so forth, and how they fit into an executive development program. That is to say, he demonstrates how the company organization, a manager's superior, and outside stimuli affect self-development. What Flippo and most of the other "self-development" advocates are saying is that self-development requires a great deal more than the "self." Ronald Shuman has pointed out "that 'development' *does* involve superiors. It is not, or should not be, wholly a matter of individual or self-development on the part of the subordinate."[63] Or, as Drucker has noted, the organizational climate, the structure, the standards, the managerial apparatus, must be so designed that they motivate the individual to self-development. That is, the organization must have systematic, focused, and purposeful self-training.[64]

General Electric defines personnel development as "the systematic training of managers and specialists to fill present and future needs of the company, to provide for further individual growth and expansion, and to perpetuate corporate existence."[65] It therefore includes programs in the functional fields—engineering, manufacturing, marketing, and finance—as well as broad programs aimed at developing an understanding of the process of managing. The programs are designed to provide a continuous flow of managers, enabling the filling of all the needs of the company.

A look at the control measurements may throw some light on the formal training programs. One approach to measuring the effectiveness of company-sponsored personnel-development programs consists of inventorying managers and functional specialists to determine where they received their training; i.e., whether they are graduates of company programs, had no organized training, or were hired from outside the company. Such inventories, taken yearly, would give some indication of coverage of company-sponsored programs. Other measurements would be to determine what and how many weak areas are found in the organization, which could have been forecast. That is to say, from forecasting corporate needs in the past, how many of these needs did the program properly fill? Another measurement of the effectiveness of personnel development programs is the degree of progress achieved by employees who were graduates of such programs.

The first step in the operation of an orderly and successful personnel development program is to determine the needs, present and future, of each part and at all levels of the company, for each management position. Such a forecast would be a master plan of manpower requirements for each department and show the department manager's own needs and the needs of other departments—which are frequently filled by interdepartmental transfers and promotions. Robert Lewis notes, "Each department would have to receive some guidance with respect to the number and quality of individuals it would be called upon to supply to other components."[66]

Figure 4-2 shows a simple manpower chart developed in 1952 for the next decade. After a more elaborate manpower schedule is developed, the next step involves the conception of plans as how to satisfy the needs—how each department will get the number of qualified managers and specialists. This entails looking at individual department development programs, overall company programs (usually sponsored by service organizations), the availability of individuals from other departments, and the desirability of hiring outside talent. When this is finished, it is up to the departments to tell the services division what its needs are from the service-sponsored programs.

Control is difficult in this area, as the objectives, the forecasts of required personnel, are future oriented, and only ten or twenty years after the fact can a program be properly evaluated.

Harold Smiddy, a great advocate of self-development, was the designer of one of General Electric's major formal development programs. He has made some interesting points worth noting on management:

First of all, we can't engraft talent and ambition onto the personality of someone who hasn't got them. But we can create a favorable climate and give guidance to the man of ability who is his own self-starter.

In the second place, the process of natural selection—the idea that the good man invariably realizes his potentialities and rises to the top or toward it—just doesn't pan out. In our case, it has produced too few managers too late.

Moreover, we think that the practice of management is ahead of its codification. We are continuing research into method and motivation for a ten or even twenty year pull. Meantime, the responsibility for developing men using the knowledge already at hand, is written into the job assignment of every GE manager.

Perhaps the most provocative—and important—idea on which we're proceeding is that managing should be regarded as a distinct type of work, with its own disciplines, its own criteria for achievement, something which is both learnable and teachable.[67]

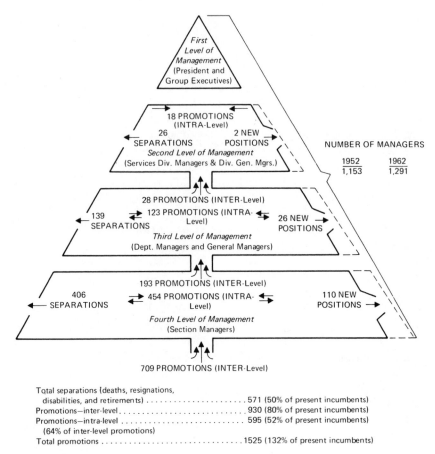

Total separations (deaths, resignations,
disabilities, and retirements) .... 571 (50% of present incumbents)
Promotions—inter-level............................ 930 (80% of present incumbents)
Promotions—intra-level .... 595 (52% of present incumbents)
(64% of inter-level promotions)
Total promotions .... 1525 (132% of present incumbents)

Figure 4-2. Analysis of Managerial Manpower Requirements for Section Manager and Higher Positions 1952 Through 1962. Source: *Professional Management in General Electric Book Three: The Work of a Professional Manager* (New York: General Electric Company, 1954), p. 99.

At General Electric it is not a major job requirement for a manager to train and develop those below him. Management development is more self-development than lead-development, although the company has an extensive system of formal training programs. The company's official policy is that "a manager has the responsibility for appraising the strengths and the weaknesses of each man who reports to him for *suggesting* 'on-the-job' and 'off-the-job' plans for *self-development* by each individual [Emphasis added]."[68]

Why is self-development emphasized, over the more traditional belief that developing subordinates is an integral part of every manager's job? After a discussion with Ralph Cordiner on November 7, 1951, Lemuel R. Boulware formally asked Harold Smiddy and Management Consultation Services to undertake a study to determine the company's needs for development of managerial manpower and to formulate a plan to meet the needs. From 1951 through 1956 Harold Smiddy led a research study into the factors that make for executive proficiency. The study was begun by informal talks with officers and managers of the company. These were followed by talks with representatives of leading corporations, by study of writings about management development, and by participation in related sessions of the American Management Association and the Society for the Advancement of Management. Then more than three hundred General Electric people were consulted covering all of the components, and finally, twenty-seven managers, from department managers and above, spent two days developing a plan of attack for the study of management development. The study then became extremely high powered, using top company executives and outside personnel. McKinsey and Company, the Psychological Corporation, and private consultants were gathered for the study. Peter Drucker and Ewing Reilley (of McKinsey) and Moorhead M. Wright (GE) headed the coordination of the study.[69] Herbert Harris, staff writer for *Nation's Business*, commented on the study:

The study also demonstrated that you can't count on a man to get ahead just because he has talent, that experience alone doesn't insure capability on the job, that management is a distinct skill, and that the practice of management is far ahead of its translation into rules and procedures.[70]

The study also brought forth the need for self-development. This is not truly self-development, for it combines self-education with management coaching and with organized training programs. It is the policy of the firm that

responsibility for manager development is accordingly a responsibility of each man as an individual and as a manager. As an individual he has the responsibility for his self-development; as a manager, he has the responsibility for the development opportunities and challenges of the men under him.[71]

Position guides for managers include responsibility for manager development as inherent in each manager's job, although not a major part of the job, and as an important consideration in evaluation of the incumbent's performance. The words *teach, advise,* and *counsel* can be found in the position guides of all managers at General Electric, including the position guide for the Chairman of the Board and Chief Executive Officer. That position guide, developed for Cordiner, states, "The primary measures of the Chairman of the Board and Chief Executive Officer's performance will be: ... The quality of managerial leadership in teaching, advising and counseling officers and General Managers."[72]

Harris termed the General Electric study "perhaps the most elaborate management development project of any in U.S. industry."[73] From the original study, extensive organized training programs were developed that are now in use at General Electric. These training programs have more than one objective. Besides the normal objective of producing competent managers and specialists for new positions and as replacements for posts vacated, the programs also seek to help the executive function more effectively in his present position and to correct any narrowness of outlook caused by overspecialization of function and provincialism of corporate background. "No company, no industry, can afford to let managers just happen,"[74] says Smiddy. To back up each department's personnel development programs, General Electric set up two programs under Smiddy's Management Consultation Services: a decentralized "Professional Business Management Course" and a centralized "General Electric Advanced Management Course." The Advanced Management Course was given at the General Electric Management Research and Development Institute at Crotonville on the Hudson, some thirty-five miles north of New York City. The company's attitude is similar to that found behind the excellent programs of Standard Oil (N.J.), Sears Roebuck, General Motors, and others. The General Electric program is much broader than other corporate programs and may be considered similar to the Harvard MBA program.

The Crotonville Management Research and Development Institute, known in the press as "General Electric U." or "GE College," is situated on the estate of the late Harry Arthur Hopf, a pioneer management consultant. The original course was designed in 1956 by such men as Smiddy, Drucker, Marc A. deFerranti, Edward Kemble, Earl Brooks, and Frank Gilmore (the latter two being the current and past directors of Cornell's Executive Development Program). Set up like an accelerated MBA program, originally the course extended for thirteen consecutive weeks, with classes meeting five and one-half days a week; the eighty executives who attended were permitted one weekend at home during the course.[75] The first semester had most of the course designers as lecturers, as well as Ralph Cordiner, Robert Paxton (GE), Dr. Lillian Gilbreth, Lemuel Boulware, Norman Maier, Gerard Swope, and Chris Argyris.[76] Other semesters have seen Lyndall Urwick, Myles Mace (Harvard), Douglas McGregor (MIT), Paul Mills and Gerald Phillippe (GE) and William Newman (Columbia).[77] The eighty students, selected by their immediate superiors, came from three levels below the president's office down to the section manager level. During the time of the course the students were completely detached from their work, with full salaries. The cost for tuition, room, and board was $2500 per man and charged against the divisional or departmental budget, ensuring that the division or department would send only those who would profit from the course.[78] In 1956, the Institute began a nine-week course with about three hundred graduates a year. By 1961, this course had a two-year backlog of nominated students.[79] Going to Crotonville became something of a status symbol; this was a consequence that the firm did not want, but it seems to have been inevitable.

The curriculum has changed greatly over the years, but it can be termed "multifunctional." Such specialized courses as finance, marketing, accounting, and so forth are left to other training programs—those within departments or those run by special staffs. The Crotonville courses concentrate on management theory and economic, social, and political issues. Originally the Institute stressed decentralization, with such specifics as how to write and interpret policies, and how to administer salary systems. By 1960 the emphasis shifted to the business environment.

In 1961 the school shut down to reorganize the curriculum. It reopened in January 1964 with new courses and a larger number of students. Hugh Estes said at the time, "It is bigger than ever, and we run more people through it."[80] The new curriculum increased the course to thirteen-weeks with five weeks on "perspective and environment," four weeks on "strategy and action for the total enterprise," and four weeks on more specific management problems.[81]

The question, for control purposes, is "Is the Institute worthwhile?" At the outset, Smiddy said,

We wouldn't be putting our money into this project if we didn't think it's going to pay off. But it will probably be five years before we know the answer for sure. One way of measuring its success will be to compare the performance of men who've attended the Institute and those who haven't. Studies made so far indicate that executives who've taken courses at Harvard and elsewhere advance much faster than those who haven't had such training.[82]

Five years later *Business Week* evaluated the Institute. "Crotonville has had no measurable impact on the quality of GE's management."[83] No explanation was given as to how this conclusion was reached, and the school is still in existence.

During its eighty-one years, General Electric has tried out every form of personnel development, from job rotation, to having personnel attend graduate schools of business, to attendance in the firm's own staff college—the first ever created by a company for the advanced education of its personnel.[84] Yet the real development is self-development, where a job is designed so that a manager learns from his work, and by proper placement, which enables the manager to stretch. "You can keep getting your feet wet around the edges of real managing just so long. Then you have to take the plunge,"[85] says Lawrence E. Walkley, General Electric General Manager.

The rigorous performance appraisal system is a major component of General Electric's development plan every six months. Every subordinate is assessed by his superior in relation to his work assignment. The work assignment requirements are spelled out in a position guide, which is more specific and detailed than the usual job descriptions. The subordinate is rated on a sliding scale (i.e., outstanding, superior, satisfactory, not yet satisfactory, unsatisfactory) for everything from technical proficiency to emotional stability under pressure. (This evaluation will be discussed more fully in the section covering control mechanisms.)

Roy Johnson, General Electric Vice President of Executive Development, points out that the Institute is very important to a manager's development, even though the company preaches self-development. Explaining how formal training fits with self-developing at General Electric, it is estimated that 90 percent of a man's career development is derived from actual work and the responsibilities derived therefrom; another 7 percent is the result of coaching on the job from his superior; and the remaining 3 percent is achieved through formal training, such as Crotonville, Professional Business Management Course, Business Training Course (Accounting, and so forth).[86]

Employee Attitudes

The Measurements Project issued its report on Key Area No. 6, employee attitudes, in January 1958.[87] This report has not been published for public consumption, but a good description of the basis of the study was published fifteen years ago by two of the collaborators.[88]

This key result area assumes that part of each manager's job is to develop a positive attitude toward the company, particularly from each of his subordinates. Since this morale or attitude leadership is inherent in each managerial responsibility, then the extent to which a manager affects the attitudes of his subordinates should be measured to determine the effectiveness of the manager. Unfortunately, attitude measurement is not easily measured in dollars, although employee attitudes will ultimately affect the balance sheet.

Robert W. Lewis and his measurements study team claim that men bring to their place of employment six specific needs which affect their attitude.

1. The need for compensation and related benefits to obtain or maintain a desired level of living.
2. The need for recognition and appreciation of his accomplishments and of the efforts he expends.
3. The need for acceptance by his associates and his community.
4. The need for opportunity to progress.
5. The need for adequate and safe facilities.
6. The need for security for himself and his family.[89]

Enlightened management theorists such as Taylor, Follett, and the Gilbreths, long before Mayo, recognized these needs, both material and nonmaterial. Reflecting the social responsibilities of business, managers have attempted to provide working conditions whereby the employees have an opportunity to satisfy their needs. The extent to which a company succeeds in meeting its social responsibility is reflected in part by the attitudes of its employees. The development of employee attitudes of active and willing cooperation, and "of wanting to direct their efforts toward the success of the enterprise,"[90] is of primary concern to the business. Brigadier General Edward L. Munson, Chief of Morale Branch, United States Army, as far back as 1921, said,

such negative factors as impatience, indifference and lack of interest reveal themselves with mathematical accuracy in the amount of product created. Morale depression thus has the same effect on the individual's productivity as physical defeat.[91]

Earl Brooks, Professor of Personnel at Cornell, says,

Surveys show that at least four out of five employees who fail to make good on the job have the knowledge and skill to do the work required but they fail because of their unsatisfactory attitudes, interests, and work habits.[92]

Although Brooks has introduced some additional factors, it can be safely stated that employee attitudes are of more than just passing interest to management.

If management is to discharge its leadership function properly, it must get information concerning the types of attitudes that exist and take the proper action that will result in attitudes favorable toward the company's objectives. To accomplish this, the measurements team attempted to:

1. Arrange information in a more orderly pattern so as to facilitate understanding;
2. Give greater assurance that all of the significant information about attitudes will be disclosed;
3. Provide a method of observing changes in attitude over a period of time;
4. Provide a means whereby the relative level of attitudes in one group or segment of an organization may be observed and compared with the level of attitudes of other groups.[93]

Using direct questioning and analysis of statistical data, General Electric developed a measuring system on employee attitudes designed to "isolate a number of broad attitude areas, measure them on a relatively uniform scale and identify them with particular segments of the organization."[94]

The statistical data to be used, in conjunction with direct questioning, relate to:

Tardiness
Absence
Resignations
Benefit Plan Participation
Accidents
Suggestions[95]

In the initial (1955) interim report, grievances and work stoppages were also used as data.[96] These data are known, collectively, as the ERI, Employee Relations Index. The various statistics used are termed indicators of employee attitudes; they reflect behavior that is optional on the part of the employees, such as absenteeism. Some absenteeism is not optional, of course—illness, court duty, family emergencies—but some absenteeism is optional, and used with other indicators, it helps to point out trends. "The behavior at the root of the statistic should have implications as being either in accord with objectives of the business or at variance with such objectives,"[97] wrote Merrihue and Katzell, two members of the study team.

Several years of work went into getting the statistics, analyzing them, testing their validity, and assigning relative weights to each factor. Using factor analysis on several sets of data covering forty plants and more than six hundred work groups, it was found that the indicators do tend to fluctuate.[98] Merrihue and Katzell add, "the sensitivity of several of the indicators in the plant-wide analysis was improved when due allowance was made for the influence of certain background variables on some of them (e.g., effects of community growth on separations rate)."[99] This is adding much subjectivity to the study.

Professor Thomas Gilson, in discussing the ERI with William C. Schwarzbek, one of the members of the Measurements Project, pointed out that the indicators used can be manipulated by managers. Using strong authoritarian threatening pressure on subordinates, absenteeism, turnover, and so forth can be cut down for short periods, although in the long run organizational deterioration is likely.[100] This has been also pointed out by many others.[101]

The other half of the employee attitude study is the attitude questionnaire. A questionnaire was developed, tested, and used by General Electric for hourly rated employees. The original study questionnaire contained fifty-six questions covering twelve categories.[102] The questions related to compensation, working conditions, various aspects of supervision, some features of group relationships, work methods, incentive climate, and value perceptions. After the survey was conducted, the managers, supervisors, and foremen received all of the information on employee attitudes, which enabled them to compare the relative standing of their groups to all other groups in the plant or department.

The two measures, statistical data and questionnaire, are at best samples of employee attitudes which give some indication of employee personal satisfactions, preferences, and evaluations, and which also indicate job-related behavior based on personnel statistics. Once the attitude survey has identified significant deviation from what the manager expects, then action can be taken. Expected attitudes are determined by long-term study to determine what is "normal" for such a group and by subjective guesswork. Each manager is to be measured by matching the results of the study against expectations, which are developed, as are other objectives, by close work between the manager and his boss.

The measurements team hoped that the attitude survey would be made each year and that it would be used to evaluate the effectiveness of past courses of action, allowing present action to be planned with better predictability. In other words, through long years of investigation and measuring of various situations and management actions, certain practices might emerge that fit the needs of each type of situation, enabling management to identify the best course of action to take for a given situation.

Public Responsibility

The seventh key result area by which all General Electric managers are to be measured is public responsibility. Drucker says, "Management is also responsible for making sure that the present actions and decisions of the business enterprise will not create future public opinion, demands and policies that threaten the enterprise, its freedom, and its economic success."[103] General Electric places great emphasis on this area: "Society's appraisal of the conduct of the Company is dependent upon the impressions received as the result of actions taken by all levels of management, including the actions of the Product Department."[104] Yet General Electric was involved in thirteen antitrust cases brought by the Department of Justice between 1940 and 1948,[105] and in late 1960 an antitrust price-fixing case involving General Electric became front-page reading, which gave American business as a whole its worst public relations of this century, perhaps of any century.

Public responsibility used as a partial measurement of a manager's ability is probably more a measurement of negative responses than of positive reactions. When public attitude is opposed to a firm, a product, or managers, and this can be ascertained through employee and public-attitude surveys, then corporate counteraction can be applied. Positive acceptance, which is expected, is not so readily noticed; hence, a manager can be adversely affected by measuring his effect on public opinion, but it is unlikely that he will be helped in his overall rating by having strong positive acceptance.

This area presents a major problem if it is used as a control device, for measuring it is difficult, even if it is a subjective measurement. Robert Lewis, in his preliminary study of this area, says:

We have tentatively concluded that responsibilities to share owners, educational institutions, and areas of government are best measured from an overall company viewpoint rather than from the viewpoint of the individual product businesses. In addition, we believe that there would be little point in trying to measure relationships with customers under the heading of "public responsibility." . . . The effectiveness of the way in which the product businesses fulfill their responsibility to their customers is best measured by "market position."[106]

Public responsibility that involves the realization that the job and the jobholder are part of a corporate body. A corporate body like General Electric is an institution, a citizen and a major factor in the society in which it lives. What society and the nation believe also has a great impact on the corporation. Large corporations are in great measure responsible for many of the great gains in our society. Society and the country are its customers, owners, and employees.

In his report on this key area, Lewis said, "We may confine ourselves to the . . . obligation of the corporation: to conduct itself as a good citizen within society."[107] This was just six years before the price-fixing case broke, and a year in which price-fixing was occurring within General Electric, according to testimony offered in the now-famous Philadelphia trial.[108]

It has been suggested by a number of people, Senator Estes Kefauver among them, that decentralization within General Electric helped to foster the price-fixing stemming from the loss of control.[109] Cordiner answered under oath, "the decentralization has nothing to do with antitrust violations."[110] Cordiner retained former President of General Electric Charles Wilson to investigate the President's Office and any other part of General Electric he wished, in an effort to determine guilt.[111] From Wilson's investigation and from other reports, the firm made extensive efforts to prevent future violations and to promote good public relations by having an educational campaign for the employees and by introducing different or additional auditing systems.[112]

Balance Between Short-Range and Long-Range Goals

The eighth and last key result area in measuring managerial ability is the ability properly to balance short-range and long-range goals. To be consistent with the listing of the various control devices used by General Electric, this eighth key area has been included in the discussion of the Measurements Project. The company has not as yet developed a research report for this area, although when it is developed it will necessarily be a highly subjective measurement. This area is, in fact, interwoven with the other seven measurement areas. Lewis says:

As a practical matter, we have decided that our approach will be to consider the "balance between short-range and long-range goals" as an integral part of the development of measurements in each of the first seven key result areas, rather than as an area separate and distinct in itself. Upon completion of the measurements program in the other seven areas, we plan to summarize the specific recommendations which relate to the proper balance between goals in order to assure ourselves that consideration has been given to this important factor.[113]

From this statement it can be deduced that any measurement in the other seven areas must consider both long-range and short-range goals, however defined.

The eighth key result area is essentially different in nature from the other seven, and might be treated as a major element of each of them.

The reports from the eight key result areas represent the foundation for further operational work measurements, functional work measurements, and managerial work measurements.

Other than a cursory look at these eight key areas, as found in the eleven pages of a Controllership Foundation booklet published in 1955, no other known discussion can be found distributed outside the company. The key to the entire control function at General Electric under decentralization is found in how these key areas are designed and administered. Employees affiliated with this project do not admit that the reports have been issued on all of the areas. It is known that each area was thoroughly investigated and highly secret reports issued which have been closely guarded by the company as high-security items. When questioned as to the availability of these reports, more than one high-ranking executive made it abundantly clear that the firm was not about to let any outsiders peer at their contents. The profitability report is considered especially private, as it contains penetrating analyses of the internal mechanisms of the company and could be competitively damaging if the report were to become publicized. Reports were issued on the following key result areas: Profitability (January 1954); Market Position (April 1956); Product Leadership (April 1956); and Employee Attitudes (January 1958). It was stated, off the record, that a key result area report has been issued within the past few years.

Measurements of the Work of Management

The four paragraphs below are all that the Measurements Project team has written to date. It is Harold Smiddy's understanding that a fifth book in the *Professional Management in General Electric* series was issued on this subject.[114] Therefore, the following is taken in whole from the Measurement Project's overall report:

Measurements in the third sub-project, the work of management, also seem to us to be contingent upon the measurements developed in the operational and functional areas. In the final analysis, the work of management must be measured in terms of actual performance in all areas in comparison with the standards set for those areas.

However, since managing is a distinct and professional kind of work, we believe that a balanced appraisal requires in effect that we back off and take a separate look at the quality of the job that has been done on planning, organizing, integrating and measuring in each of the Key Result Areas. If this kind of appraisal is performed separately, we feel that the chance of obtaining a balanced, fair, and objective evaluation is considerably enhanced.

At this point, it appears that the most useful device for measuring the work of management is of a qualitative nature, that is, a check list of questions directed at pinpointing strengths and weaknesses under each of the elements of management. Such questions must be constructed within the broad background of actual results in the operational and functional areas and must be designed to evaluate the work of a management team in a given business or a given function rather than the work of an individual manager.

This approach to measuring the work of management could be used effectively immediately following a Business Review, when the Reviewer would have at hand specific evidence on which to base his appraisal. If it is agreed that the most important areas of business performance are those that we have referred to as the Key Result Areas, presumably each business should be planning, organizing, integrating and measuring its activities—short and long range—in terms of these areas. The Business Review, in turn, should then be constructed around the Key Result Areas so that how well the management work has been performed can be evaluated in the light of actual accomplishments.[115]

Functional Measurements

Functional measurements comprise one of the three subprojects organized to formulate a workable measurement or control system. Functional measurements include the work of manufacturing, marketing, financial, and all of the staff functions, such as engineering, employee relations, community relations, and legal. It was expected that the eight key result areas, which constituted the operational measurement subproject, would form the basis on which to build sound measurements of the functional work and the work of management. This has yet to be proven.

The Measurements Project has concentrated its efforts on exploring the eight key result areas under Operational Measurements, and therefore little has been done to formulate functional measurements other than those which come about through the day-to-day operations of any of the various functional components. Basically, General Electric has concluded that one way of getting at the answers is to analyze each function along these lines:

1. What are the objectives of the function in terms of the business as a whole, or what should the General Manager expect from each function?
2. What are the objectives of each function in terms of the other functions, or what should the General Manager expect each function to contribute to the other functions?[116]

What is expected by General Electric is that each function should be analyzed to see how it relates to others; this analysis should be made by functional specialists working with representatives from the other functions.

It was anticipated by the Measurements Project team that measurements of functional work will be and are highly qualitative in nature.[117] Subjective evaluation—or, more bluntly, "guessed-at evaluation"—is the method of measuring functional effectiveness. In advancing this viewpoint of functional measurements, it might appear that the measurements project goal of better measurements has not progressed significantly because of the suggestion to rely heavily on the exercise of judgment. Robert Lewis's team replies,

In our opinion, measurements are designed to supplement judgment, not supplant it. They help to ask the right questions but seldom give answers in themselves. By thinking through the objectives of the functions and establishing for ourselves what we expect a given function to do for the General Manager and for the other functions, we will develop measurements that are just as valid as numerical indexes. We should continue our efforts to develop quantitative measurements but always with the recognition that even quantitative measurements require the exercise of judgment.[118]

The hand that guides the pen of objectivity is most subjective.

Budgets

The method of planning and budgeting and the means for measuring and controlling are considered by many as keys for seeing the difference between "real" decentralization and "lip service" decentralization. John Flowers, Manager of Business Analysis and Cost Accounting Consulting, sees decentralization from the point of view of how industrial budgets are set and measured. He reports that during Swope's reign and by the early thirties, an Appropriation and Budget Committee was organized, which consisted of the President and six staff and seven department heads.[119] This committee reviewed the operations of all staff areas and operations of the firm. Flowers claims that the firm had little consolidation of total budgets other than that prepared by the committee from data provided by each department for use in budget reviews. There was no regular required consolidation of budgets in advance of the committee's review; reports of the total company budget were prepared when requested or as summarized by the Appropriation and Budget Committee. He says there was no detailed breakdown by account and by function—at least in the modern accounting sense. During the thirties and forties, each foreman was given an expense budget broken down by month and by account. This budget did not include items received from central purchasing. Flowers indicated the budget was developed at the top of the operating organization (usually the department or plant) and reviewed with the operating vice president and ultimately with the Appropriation and Budget Committee. On some occasions, the committee changed proposed budgets and directed the operating vice president to revise his plans accordingly. After a budget was agreed upon, it was broken down by operating activity and each department or plant manager would assign portions of the budget to his subordinates, ultimately reaching each foreman. This is known as centralized or top-down budgeting. "Foremen were handed a budget; they had to live within it," says Flowers, "and they had to explain variances."[120]

Decentralization changed top-down budgeting. In 1953, position guides or descriptions began to be written and formulated for all managerial jobs within the organization. These guides stated the responsibility by defining the job, and therefore made the jobholder accountable for results. It was now possible to use bottoms-up budgeting. The budget became a joint effort between the manager responsible for results and his supervisor. Total acceptance and implementation of bottoms-up budgeting took about five years, according to Flowers. Bottoms-up budgeting was a great change and allowed decentralization to become a reality, as well as a philosophy.

Under bottoms-up budgeting, each manager working with his supervisor developed his own budget. Because it was his own, it was expected he would try harder to live within it. The manager was held accountable for the results of his own designed budget and any variances would be carefully scrutinized. He was graded on the proper fit of his output against budgeted output, justifying any variances. In instances where the environment had changed more than antici-pated, managers sometimes even had to explain why they were within the budget.

After decentralization, the department level became the point for evaluation on a profit-and-loss basis; each department was a profit center. Therefore, the manager of a department must budget so that he can produce the best profit or least possible loss. Under the previous organization, there were fewer profit-and-loss centers and the aggregation of activities within a center would involve many plants and products. Purchasing was centralized for the profit-and-loss center and there was no profit-and-loss evaluation at the plant or product line level. As a result, a plant manager's operating budget would not include allocations for centralized purchases—which meant that items from central purchasing were not budgeted and not charged against the lower-level managers. Consequently, if two items were needed from central purchasing, three would be ordered. The desire to have extras ready was rationalized by the fact that the extra, and often unused, material did not "cost" the manager or foreman, but if his workers ruined some of the material and were held up waiting for replacements, the budgeted time allowed for completion of that job would be higher than expected and would cause a variance.

Beginning in 1949, purchasing was decentralized, with each plant handling its own purchases. This gradual takeover by departments of purchasing became complete by 1953. With the decentralization of purchasing came the concept of "profit centers." Each department, being a "profit center," was evaluated on its profit or loss. This meant that purchasing at the department level could greatly affect the profit or loss of each department. No longer could a manager allow his foreman to "overpurchase" materials just to play it safe. Now when two items were needed only two items were ordered. Each foreman now was evaluated, among other methods, by how effective or efficient he was with the goods with which he had to work—including what he ordered. Consequently, department managers wanted to hold down unneeded purchases to raise profits or lower losses, and foremen could not overbudget because it would make them look inefficient with their inputs.

The concept of bottoms-up budgeting means that budgeting became an operating function rather than a staff function. When budgeting was top-down, budgets were developed by the top operating management of plants utilizing their staffs. With bottoms-up budgeting, budgets were developed by each manager starting at the foreman level, and these budgets were integrated into the budget of the next higher level. This is budgeting being initiated by the operating personnel, and in each case having the authority commensurate with the responsibility.

For clarity, it must be added that when each department level was considered as a profit center (in 1951), each department was naturally given pricing responsibility. It would have been irrational to consider a department as a profit-loss center without pricing responsibility.

Flowers notes that from 1950 to 1958 all budgets were proposed in constant dollars. In 1957-58, budgeting changed to current dollars to enable a more realistic figure to be presented.

The budget is the prime control mechanism for day-to-day operations. It allows the rapid identification of any variances in plans which must be explained. Thus, quick adjustments can be initiated.

Most department budgets are derived ultimately from sales forecasts. Managers in manufacturing can figure their production from sales forecasts, thus being able to budget their needs. Of course, this is not the only method of budgeting, nor should it be implied that all budgets are in dollars alone. A look at the eight key result areas makes it obvious that managers at General Electric use numerous types of budgets and are measured against each of these budgets. Some of these budgets are less quantitative, and therefore require more subjective judgment than some other types.

As Manager of Business Analysis and Cost Accounting Consulting, Flowers made the following observations as to the role of the Corporate accounting organization. Corporate accounting recommends formats to be used by each department. These recommendations are developed with the aid of each department. In developing the formats, consideration must be given to the type of financial data normally available and to the requirements of corporate executives for information needed to evaluate and approve budgets. These recommendations, however, are not requirements. The gathering of information and, to some extent, the presentation of the information is a function of each individual department. Corporate accounting must, of course, define requirements for particular types of information such as that needed for federal income tax and federal securities regulations reporting, and for consistency in external reporting. Within these requirements and the specification of accounting principles, each department develops an accounting system designed for its particular peculiarities. Above the department level, information is presented in summary form and much conformity may be detected, as there are only about ten basic groups in the firm. Each group's vice president may require special information, but for practical purposes they all end up asking for similar data. Flowers again emphasizes that budget control is in the line, not in staff. Corporate accounting only helps, it does not dictate; it gathers information that the line asks it to gather. Therefore, budgeting control and reporting is performed by those who have line responsibility for individual products. Whereas in the 1940s corporate accounting basically maintained general accounting, cost accounting, personnel accounting, tax accounting, and auditing, its function has been expanded to include budgeting, measurement, data processing and information systems. These are areas in which corporate accounting gives assistance to an operating department which requests help.

The final budget for each department must be prepared by December of the preceding year. The long-range forecast cycle begins early in the year, so that a profit-and-loss component will have developed estimates of sales volume and its direct cost for the next five years by the end of April of the previous year. The five-year forecast will include a preliminary budget, but this is refined and adjusted in a series of reviews beginning in midyear to completion in December of a final operating budget for the year. Thus, General Electric requires each department to budget up to five years ahead.[121]

Capital budgeting is centralized which is to say that commitments over $500,000 could not be made at the Operating Department level by general managers.[122] The Policy (No. 20.6) for Investments in Facilities lists the following dollar expenditure which may be made without higher approval, as follows:

Dollar Appropriations	*Lowest Sole Authority to Grant Approval*
1. $500,000 or more	1. Board of Directors
2. Below $500,000	2. Group Executive, Chief Executive Officers, President, Chairman of the Board

Dollar Appropriations	*Lowest Sole Authority to Grant Approval*
3. Below $250,000	3. Division General Manager or at equivalent level, Services Officers
4. Below $100,000	4. One level above the delegated approval for operations meeting criteria[1 2 3]

The consensus, as stated by John Flowers, is that bottoms-up or true decentralized budgeting was started about 1953, a reversal of centralized top-down budgeting of earlier years. It was also a change from staff budgeting as practiced by the Appropriation and Budget Committee to line budgeting as practiced by each department. Paul Mills, who had over thirty years' service with General Electric (part of this time as Manager—Finance for the Air Conditioning Division, and twelve years as Manager of Organization Consulting Service), believes that most of the above information is more propaganda than fact. He says, "as far back as 1930 to 1932, I had a job in General Expense in Headquarters disbursements to help company budget officers put budgets together from all over the company. The underlying work was done by departments—those responsible for results."[1 2 4]

Conclusion

Over forty years ago, Mary Parker Follett pointed out the need for the type of control which General Electric already used. She said in a lecture delivered in London in 1932:

The ramifications of modern industry are too wide-spread, its organizations too complex, its problems too intricate for it to be managed by commands from the top alone. This being so, we find that when central control is spoken of, that does not mean a point of radiation, but the gathering of many controls existing throughout the enterprise.[1 2 5]

This chapter has presented a number of measuring devices developed by General Electric. The use of eight key result areas as part of the evaluation for profit centers, the first industrial use of MBO as we understand the term today, and the intense study of management techniques for all managers are perhaps unsurpassed by any other organization. To totally understand the sophistication developed to control decentralization by GE in the 1950s, much of what was developed then is just now entering the text books in the 1970s. The key to the control is the development of self-control, whereby delegation of authority becomes more than lip service—it is real. Equally important is the development of measurements which enable the measured to evaluate himself and to be evaluated on items which are important to the success of the organization and to avoid being measured against irrelevant standards.

5 The Environment of Decentralization

This chapter covers General Electric's organizational evolution from a centralized functionalization to a decentralization by product lines, in theory as well as in practice—it concentrates on some problems, particularly people problems, associated with decentralization. The chapter is organized into two sections, but each is intertwined with the other, forming what might be termed "the General Electric environment." The breakdown into two sections is used to enable an easier understanding by dissecting the system and allowing a look at some of its components. Although synergism may be lost by this method, it does help research and presentation and, it is to be hoped, comprehension. The first section deals with "The Organization Structure," as it influenced the people in the organization. The second section, "Control," focuses on the use of "Measurements"; "the One-result Area"; and "Management By Objectives."

The theoretical foundation upon which the General Electric Company's management and organization philosophy was established was firmly laid down in documents prepared by its Management Consultation Services. Although the philosophy was thought through and painstakingly implemented, the course followed by the organization was not without problems. For it is people who man, organize, and run an organization. No human organization is perfect, and an organization the size of General Electric has to reckon with the considerable differences of ability, temperament, and integration among people. Charles E. Wilson, who was President of General Electric before the decentralization philosophy was implemented, is said to have had an outstanding personal charisma which helped him to run an $800 million company. Ralph Cordiner is said to have had "as much charisma as a cold fish," yet he ran the firm at five times the size. The stated philosophy and organization structure of the firm was of necessity styled to give the individual as much leeway as possible, which often allowed the idiosyncrasies of individuals to play havoc with the system. Frequently, it has been found that some of the philosophy itself does not seem to reflect the goals of the organization. For instance, it can be stated that General Electric goals are long range—for profit in the long run—yet the control mechanisms employed tend to force managers to emphasize the short run. This point will be expanded in this chapter.

Philip D. Reed, who was Chairman of the Board under both Wilson and Cordiner, says that the two men were quite different, and consequently the type of organization structure required by the company during their reigns had to be greatly dissimilar. "Charley Wilson was an old-time operator who had never been

97

in a truly decentralized operation." (The only truly decentralized area before 1950 was Lamps.) "This was all right for the 1920s and thirties," says Reed. "We weren't so damn big and complex. We could work with reasonable effort that was [highly centralized]."[1] Cordiner, on the other hand, was termed "a student of organization theory"[2] by Reed. The organizational problems did not seem too serious in the period before World War II, but Reed remembers,

As we emerged from there the fact we were going to be a billion dollar company overnight struck us. We both [Wilson and Reed] could see a major management problem, not only in dollars but in products—chemical, aircraft, and so forth. We had to do a major job of breaking down an amorphous organization. An organization whose top men were split between New York and Schenectady. We needed a major study of organization and Ralph Cordiner was the best man for that. He spent at least two years doing nothing else other than study the General Electric organization."[3]

Cordiner brought Harold F. Smiddy to New York to plan the new organization. Smiddy came to be perhaps the most feared man in the company, while at the same time considered by most who knew him the most brilliant management theorist in the corporation. As many past managers observed, "you either liked him or hated him; there was no middle of the road. You had to respect his brilliance." Smiddy formulated the basic concepts and the organization building blocks about 1951, but few claim that the concept was really working effectively until 1958 or 1960. Smiddy confirms that true decentralization was only beginning to take place at the time of his retirement in 1960.[4] One major reason for this slow attainment of goals was the fact that General Electric had an enormous number of strong-charactered managers at the vice-president level. These men blocked many changes and usually didn't want "to give up the business"—that is, they did not want to let go of the reins, the right to personally direct those profit centers which were removed from one to two levels below them in the department. These strong men did not willingly release power to their departments, and thus held up true decentralization in practice. Yet Drucker, sounding like the realist he is rather than a purist, believes some managers must buck the rules of decentralization once in a while, although perhaps not to the extent found in General Electric. He says,

For decentralized management to be efficient, it must contain at least a sprinkling of executives who pay very little attention to the rules of decentralization and are inclined toward a rather autocratic "do-this-or-be-damned" attitude. . . . High-handed, arbitrary, even dictatorial behavior may thus be not only no contradiction to decentralization but a prerequisite for its functioning, provided only that such behavior is seen and understood by everybody . . . as an exception and as a deviation from the norm.[5]

Unfortunately, in General Electric the old guard outnumbered the disciples of the new philosophy and were more than just a sprinkling.

General Electric decentralization required an explosive increase in the size of middle management.[6] In 1953, the firm predicted that by 1962 the total employment of the company would be 300,000 employees, of whom 108,000 would be salaried and 192,000 hourly employees.[7] In 1962, actual employment was only 258,000.[8] The 1953 estimate was 20 percent over the actual requirements of the firm. The error in estimating projected employment for 1962 was caused by the underestimation of future productivity. It had been assumed that the company would produce $5 billion in sales in 1962, and this estimate was very close to the actual sales of $4.8 billion.[9] This means that the productivity per employee was far greater in 1962 than had been calculated.

In the early years of decentralization, sweeping reorganizations of the company were accomplished, but not without a great deal of turnover in employment. With new prime responsibility pushed down on lower-level managers, most of whom had not experienced such a burden, many were found not qualified to handle the responsibility, because of either inability or lack of desire to accept such responsibility. The first years from 1954 to 1958, immediately following the delegation of authorities demanded by the decentralization structure, were disrupted internally because of this high turnover rate. The turnover rate for managerial jobs at this or any other period has not been released; Vice Chairman Jack S. Parker says the turnover rate was high then but asserts it leveled off after 1958 and is currently not a major problem.[10]

It took quite a few years and much friction before General Electric evolved from a centralized functional organization to one structured on decentralized product lines. When Cordiner was asked why this was so, he replied:

For one thing, I thought that a lot of the fellows we took from functional jobs and made general managers would respond to the challenge of being measured. I was wrong. I should have realized that you can't expect a fellow who has been running just a part of it to, all of a sudden, be accountable for the whole thing.

In fact, to my surprise, a lot of people who looked good in functional jobs actually asked to be passed by. They didn't want to stick their necks out. A lot of these people and some others came to me and said, "See all the troubles you've caused and the heartaches." Okay, but if I hadn't the company couldn't have gone from $2 billion to $5 billion—and now it's $7.2 billion.[11]

The Organization Structure

The picture usually painted by present and past employees of General Electric is one of outstanding achievement in the organizational areas. Yet some dissent is found among practitioners when they are pressed to describe what changes occurred in the actual day-to-day operations, as opposed to what was changed on paper. Paul Mills, who was Manager—Organization Consulting Service when he resigned in 1962, when asked what really changed in terms of control, said, "I don't think a damn thing changed. They [General Electric] never lost centralized financial control; it was there before and is there today."[12] Mills had an excellent vantage point to see the control mechanisms in the firm. At the time of his retirement, he was the highest-paid non-vice-president in the company. His boss, Harold F. Smiddy, was Vice President of Management Consultation Services, and it was the Smiddy team that engineered the organization restructuring from 1950 through 1961. Mills began his association with General Electric in the early twenties and concentrated in Finance, and ended with Management Consultation Services.

It is Mills's opinion that Cordiner and Smiddy didn't effectively achieve any real control changes, other than the reorganization of the lines on the chart. He believes they "didn't because of the power struggle wherein about a quarter of a million workers were led by powerful executives in four or five of the main areas [both operational and functional]."[13] These strong leaders chose and developed their own select group of extremely loyal, highly intelligent managers. Their loyalty was not to the Company, as Cordiner and Smiddy hoped. Mills did not say, but others, being assured of anonymity, emphasized that Cordiner feared most of these strong "characters" who headed up the larger operational groups and functional areas, such personalities as Henry Erben, head of Major Apparatus, and Robert Paxton, of Large Transformers, and Walter Baker of Radio, Television and Electronics. Many claim Cordiner had hoped to break down the internal power structured of these men but failed to do so. Cordiner, it must be remembered, was considered an outsider. He did not come up through the ranks in General Electric. Cordiner came from Edison General Electric Appliance Company in 1932 and left in 1939 to become President of Schick. After war service he again went to work for General Electric as Assistant to the President, at a considerable decrease in pay,[14] and he headed up the Wilson organization evaluation.[15] At 570 Lexington Avenue (Corporate headquarters of General Electric) he was referred to as the "undertaker" or "hatchetman." He was also considered a loner by those at the top of the organization. Mills believes Cordiner used Smiddy to head the reorganization because Smiddy was a powerful figure by sheer personality and knowledge. But Mills comments,

Cordiner failed because the reorganization could not break up the loyalty [to particular managers] within the areas. He was unable to redirect this loyalty which had developed over many years to a new managing philosophy called professional management.[16]

Having managers think of themselves as "professional" was one goal of the decentralization; the firm's famous four books on management are called *Professional Management in General Electric,* and Cordiner's own book is called *New Frontiers for Professional Managers.* There was great effort to try to make the work of managing objective oriented and to break away from past loyalties and narrower viewpoints both in the operational and functional areas.

In a move to destroy much of the power structure of the Comptroller's Office, Cordiner made Harold A. MacKinnon (head of the powerful Auditing component in Comptroller's Division) Manager of the Component Products Division in 1952, and in 1953 he moved the Comptroller, Donald Millham, to manage the Lamp Division. This allowed Cordiner to place a hand-picked ally, Gerald L. Phillippe, as head of the highly feared and powerful Comptroller's Department. Much later, Cordiner promoted Phillippe to President (1961), and at Cordiner's retirement, Phillippe became Chairman of the Board. It is interesting to note that these moves did not lessen or change the built-in loyalties of the Comptroller's staff, merely shifting their allegiance to Phillippe and not to the philosophy.[17]

To see how and why the Comptroller's Office was so powerful and exercised such tight control, we must look at its role in the firm. Traditionally in General Electric the Comptroller is head of Accounting Services and reports to the President. The Treasury Department is a totally different organization, and throughout the fifties the Treasurer reported to the Chairman of the Board. Within the last five years the Accounting and Treasury Departments have been combined to form Corporate Finance reporting to the Corporate Executive Office. However, before the combination the Comptroller and his Accounting Services were, in company lingo, called the Financier and Finance Department. These titles did not refer to the Treasurer and were not used officially. It was the Comptroller rather than the Treasurer who planned and determined many of the control mechanisms. The Finance Department, as a Service component, had the right and obligation to audit its counterpart in each of the operational groups and divisions. That is to say, the Comptroller's Office as a staff or service organization would audit the financial statements and financial component of each product or line group. The Financial Department had this right from the early 1930s, as far as those interviewed could remember, and most likely well before that. At least during the early thirties the Financial Department sent out teams of traveling auditors to every department, visiting once a year and more often in the larger areas. Therefore, it can be stated that from the 1930s forward General Electric had two financial departments; the Comptroller's Department, with its traveling auditors, and the financial staff attached to each product group or line. The financial staff attached to each product group or division was responsible to the manager of the product line and not to the Comptroller and his accounting organization—at least, this was the stated structure. It was hoped that the two financial organizations would be independent of each other and serve as double checkpoints, each checking the product department figures and conformance to accounting policies and practices. But this was not how it worked in practice.

In the thirties and forties the audit staff from the finance area as well as the audit staff from the product groups would compare the budgeted or planned expenditure with the actual. More will be said on how this budget was developed shortly. Any variances from plans, when discovered by the Comptroller's staff, would be duly noted and filtered to top-level management through the Comptroller's Office. Thus, the financial fraternity was respected for ability and feared for results stemming from their visits. The Comptroller had the ear of both the President (Swope, Wilson, or Cordiner) and the Chairman of the Board (Young or Reed). This is one method by which the Comptroller exercised control and power.

The Financial Fraternity

A second source of control and power came through what most call the "financial fraternity." The Comptroller and his associates had the right of appointment (before 1951) or veto (after 1951) of *any* financial manager in any department to assure that the prospective financial manager did meet the standards of the Comptroller. Unfortunately, these standards were not always explicitly stated. One standard was that the manager be a graduate of the firm's Schenectady, New York, Business Training Course, known as BTC. The course, a three-year study of accounting, is considered by General Electric to be the toughest accounting program in the country. Mills says, "Ninety-nine percent of the financial managers in departments were BTC students [graduates]."[18] Graduates of BTC had been indoctrinated with one accounting philosophy, that of the Comptroller's Department. Graduates found kinship through this common accounting philosophy and BTC. They are, therefore, acting more as a second team of financial auditors for the Comptroller than for their department. It is Mills's opinion that this practice has not been altered in recent years. The centralization-to-decentralization reorganization did not change this type of control. According to Mills, "Nothing changed, the same guys with the same background, BTC graduates, ran the financial end of the business, no matter if they were found in the corporate staff or department staff."[19] It should be noted that when Cordiner moved Donald Millham to Lamps in 1953, he replaced him with a man considered to be in the Cordiner camp, Gerald Phillippe, who was also a BTC graduate. "It [the financial fraternity] was a tight little lodge," comments Mills. "You got into it by being recruited and got out by not keeping your nose clean."[20] You could also be forced out for incompetency, as the standards set by the Comptroller were extremely high.[21]

Soon after Cordiner introduced the first moves toward implementing his reorganization plan in 1951, a conference was held in Atlantic City. It was here that the concept of the separation of "Service" and "Operating" work was introduced to managers just below the executive-vice-president level. The managers in attendance were totally unprepared for any such development. It was explained to them that the six components, where the overall responsibility for profits was then found, were to be restructured and that profit responsibility was to be assigned to approximately one hundred departments and a few sections well below the executive vice president level. It was specifically put forth that the operating unit was to be the Product Department, with its designed product field, its own personnel, its own shops, its own marketing responsibility, and its own requirements to "finance" and control its business, facilities, payroll, and related programs, procedures, and activities.

Similarly it was explained, but "considerably less clearly in many quarters and many respects," says Smiddy, that

there was developing appreciation that the work and personnel of each Services Division should increasingly be organized and subdivided to provide specialists and skilled services in each of the principal subfunctional areas, which together comprise the fundamental kind of work in which a particular Services Division is expert.[22]

It was late in 1951, after this Atlantic City conference, that the principles of decentralization began to be applied in practice. But decentralization or reorganization of such a huge complex organization took time. When Wilson abruptly left General Electric, Cordiner was faced with the choice of implementing decentralization slowly or quickly. He chose the quick overhaul—he expected the application and acceptance of the principles of decentralization to take only five years.[23] Five years, although considered the shortest possible time for reorganization, is a long time to keep an organization "hanging." It was during this period that many managers could and did complain that they heard one philosophy ("decentralization") expounded from top management but saw and felt a different concept (centralization and tight top control) from the same top level. The older managers, many of whom were found at upper levels of the new Services components, had grown up under a centralized, functionalized structure. Because of their backgrounds, many managers acted contrary to the requirements of the corporate written policies. Lower-level managers, found in the Operating components, could rightfully believe that the real intent of the Services managers was

not to let the decentralized manager act with discretion and judgment but really to recapture a piece of his delegated function as a "manager" and bring it back into a centralized Services Division area either for decision or for performance.[24]

Because of this type of action, thousands of intelligent middle supervisory and managerial men concluded that there was a lot of double talk going on.

When Cordiner first tried to delegate the authority for so many acts to the department general managers, he tried to do it before written policies on the subject were developed. Thus, in the early stages of decentralization, there were no written rules stating what authority was delegated to whom and when.

Smiddy was assigned the responsibility to see to it that such policies and badly needed position descriptions were written. This project was to take about five years before it was reasonably completed (it is a continuing project). Smiddy relates that at the outset of the project many of the executive vice presidents did not want to put their job descriptions, their authorities and responsibilities, on paper. They were reluctant to formulate the guides and policies into written statements, but decentralization would have been impossible in General Electric without the scope of each position being properly understood.

Smiddy tells about one executive vice president who was extremely powerful because of his position and personality. This man, with forty-odd years' service, could and did manage "by the seat of his pants," and was strongly against the formulation of written organized policies and position guides. After much discussion with Smiddy he sat down and wrote the most detailed, complete position description turned in by any manager, leaving nothing out and making sure that he got on paper all of his authorities and responsibilities. It needed no change, Smiddy observed, while the position descriptions of other managers in favor of the project took many months and many drafts to complete in accordance with the requirement.[25] The early position descriptions were intentionally "too detailed" because of the need to convey the philosophy while it was concurrently being formulated. Many managers refused to believe that they had the responsibilities and authorities intended and that the position description was one vehicle used to indoctrinate them.

One of the reasons for decentralizing the company was the hope to lower costs by sharpening communications. Cordiner felt that the corporation was too big to allow communications to operate through centralized organization channels. Decentralization would, he felt, free up communications between those who have information and those who need it. Without doubt, one of the biggest obstacles to effective operating management was, and still is, the imperfect status of human communication. Cordiner believed that communications should not follow the lines of an organization chart and centralization encouraged that practice.

Clash of Cultures

The first decade of decentralization (1951-60) produced a clash of cultures. The "old-school" managers' automatic reactions to situations were developed into habit patterns long before decentralization started. These people, usually found in the "power" positions of upper-level management, were on one side of the cultural clash. The other side was comprised of the younger middle-management people, who were schooled in the human-relations movement which was very much a fad during the decade of the fifties. Many of these people devoted hours of deep thought and posed many penetrating questions on the real meaning of the "new philosophy." It became increasingly difficult for these young crusaders in the new philosophy to communicate effectively with the "old-school" managers whose habits were generated prior to decentralization. According to Smiddy, although Cordiner had expected that decentralization could be complete on paper within five years after he initiated moves to reorganize, he did not expect the incumbent top managers ever to really accept it in practice, and believed that a thorough education program directed at middle management was needed to lay the groundwork by which the philosophy would slowly become accepted. Cordiner believed that only when the then middle managers accepted a true decentralized philosophy and they in turn filtered to the top would real decentralization of decision-making become a reality. Smiddy says that this was beginning to take place at the time of his retirement in 1960, nine years after the Atlantic City conference.[26]

This clash of cultures during the 1950s often "split right across an Operating Department, separating one layer of management from another or one part of a management team from the rest of the management team,"[27] says Don Webb, a member of Mills's staff and a member of the younger pro-Cordiner side of the clash. In those departments so torn, a period of inefficiency and high overhead costs must have resulted, caused in part by the fact that communication costs must have risen.

John Flowers, looking back on company history, believes it took five years (1951-56) to implement decentralization.[28] Ralph Cordiner said in 1956, "I personally felt in 1951 that five years would be required to evolve the new structure and have it implemented with understanding and enthusiasm. The program appears to be just about on schedule."[29] Therefore, 1957-58 should have been a period by which decentralization was firmly established. Donald R. Webb, who began his General Electric career in 1951 and spent many years as a manager reporting to a Department General Manager, was able to comment in 1957,

If, in keeping with the new philosophy, we are to establish high standards of performance against which we can measure our progress, it is evident that we still have a very long way to go before we can say that decentralization is working in a truly satisfactory manner.[30]

"In some areas," Paul Mills says, "it worked, they believed in it, others paid lip service to it."[31] Unfortunately, there is no nonauthoritarian way to force a manager to modify or avoid authoritarian practices, and authoritarian management has no place in General Electric's decentralized management philosophy. "[Only] through training over time will a boss see that the authoritarian way is wrong," says Mills. "[Only then will] they learn to lead with authority of knowledge rather than lead with authority of position—it is a new way of life."[32]

The conflicts generated by the many pressures on managers, especially those in operating departments which were the profit centers, and also generated by the fact that authoritarian managers existed side by side with those dedicated to the new philosophy, caused many of the "old-school" managers who did not believe in giving up authority, did not understand how it worked, or could not believe that they acted differently from what they preached, to give lip service to decentralization without in fact adopting it. Acceptance of the new philosophy had the backing of most of the corporate leaders—being the main thrust of the Advanced Management Course at Crotonville—and was coupled with a vigorous campaign in the Professional Business Management Course within all the departments of the firm. The new philosophy had to be either adopted in fact or the manager must give lip service to it.

As late as 1957, Donald Webb, then a manager in an operating department, made the following notes on this problem:

A manager is confronted with the conflict between Operating business pressures and the requirement for low overhead costs on the one hand and he must demonstrate that his department is appropriately equipped with position guides, functional charts, structural charts, and other similar paper work symbolic of the new philosophy. An enormous amount of paper work is then generated by lifting verbatim phrases and paragraphs from the Services functional charts, generic position guides for Operating Division General Manager, Operating Department General Manager and even the position guide for the President. The phrases and paragraphs which are lifted are applied in wholesale fashion to organization components and positions through the departments regardless of the real meaning or intent of these phrases. Since the phrases are lifted from sources of unquestioned authority their very application to the lower level components and positions is presumed to bring a form of sanctity like sprinkling with holy water. It is hoped that by this magic the organization will "meet the criteria," appropriate delegations will be given for making all future decisions not more than two layers above the place affected and from that time on the department will live in a new utopia of complete freedom.[33]

The writing of position guides for every position in General Electric was under the direction and coordination of Harold Smiddy and the Management Consultation Services. Position guides or the narrower written job descriptions were not found in written form before this 1951 project was started. The basic underlying principle of a position guide is to have a complete and thorough understanding between man and manager of the requirements of his position and how its performance is to be measured. It is imperative that every word and phrase in the position guide have a meaning significant to that man and his manager, a meaning that is fully understood by them and one that they believe most precisely describes the responsibilities of the position. The position guide was designed to be a working document between man and manager. But "many of the position guides existing in operating departments today, however, are not working documents,"[34] says one manager, reporting to a department general manager after about a decade following the reorganization. He went on to say,

[The position guides] are supposed by both man and manager to be full of some kind of magic gobbledygook. When it becomes necessary for them to sit down and agree on what the man is supposed to be doing, they both find it necessary to discard the position guides and start afresh in an entirely different language.[35]

Donald Webb claimed in 1957 that the same problem which occurred with position guides plagued the functional organization charts, a claim that has been repeated by managers to this day.

Many of the functional organization charts [were] . . . prepared to "meet the criteria" and it is pathetic to observe that much of this paper work has been generated solely for the principles of meeting criteria and has never become the working document in the actual organizing process that it is intended to be.[36]

The principal purpose of a functional organization chart is to show the functions and subfunctions necessary to accomplish the objectives of the overall business of the organization. Thus, the functional organization chart may be considered as a condensed, topical summary of the position guides for all of the positions in the organization, thus producing an overall "picture" of the functions and work of the organization. Hence, any complaints issued against the position guides would naturally be applicable to the functional organization chart.

In general, while the chart shows enough information to increase the understanding of all people within the component as to the relationship of this work to the whole organization structure, it also is useful to a manager external to the business, in enabling him to understand the work of each principal component and position in the organization depicted by such a chart. The functional organization chart summarizes the position guides to determine what the objectives and the work or contribution expected from a component, activity, or position really are. From it, General Electric believes one can determine to what extent major gaps or overlaps occur in the structure.[37]

The work of human relations researchers has for years demonstrated the power of the informal organization to effect the formal operation. The "financial fraternity," the "strong characters," and the "cultural clash" were strong influences on the practice, structure, and operations of General Electric. How people interpret written policy also influences the operating practices. The next section will concentrate on one of the major problems found in General Electric in this area.

Control

Measurements

Judging from the memories of the men interviewed and from attempts to read between the lines of various company publications, there seemed to be, prior to 1960, a widespread belief in General Electric that the only real measurement of performance of the operating department manager was in short-term-profit dollars. If this was true, then there was need for some strong motivation of managers to have them make any decisions that would decrease their short-run profits and yet might be necessary to meet the long-range goals of the company.

By 1970 enough material had been circulated on the eight key result areas of measurements, as covered in Chapter 4, dating back as early as January 1954,[38] and enough discussion of them had taken place, to make all managers fully knowledgeable of each of the other seven areas. Despite this knowledge, many managers were skeptical about the practicability of their application to the daily work. Donald Webb described it this way:

The general feeling is that it is all good theory [eight Key Result Areas] but when the chips are down and their bosses are actually making a determination affecting their compensation or their survival, there will be only one measurement that counts and it will be the figure at the bottom of their profit-and-loss statement.[39]

As a result of this feeling that short-run profitability was the only real measurement, many department general managers took "selfish action," in terms of the component or department, in order to add profitability to their particular departments, at the expense of the overall interest of the General Electric Company. All members of management were acquainted with the corporate policy on this subject as laid down by Cordiner, Harold Smiddy, Robert Lewis, and others as to the unprofessionalism of department selfishness. Yet when challenged by colleagues and other managers as to the correctness of pushing for profits at the expense of other areas, a typical comeback might have been:

When I see some actual signs of somebody measuring my performance or my department by my contribution to the Company as a whole, I may act differently; but as long as I am being judged by the figure on the bottom of that profit and loss sheet, I am going to make it just as big as I can and to hell with the rest of the Company.[40]

Component selfishness caused by the short run one key result area measurement caused rifts between different components of the company. If one department can increase its profitability at the expense of another department, a rift will naturally result. This happened on more than one occasion. Once the rift took place the two components could not get together objectively, since discussions were now subjective in nature. Two rival camps thus developed, each with the objective of "beating out the other unit." Much of the effort devoted to teamwork for the purposes of furthering the interests of these new opposing camps turned out to be nonproductive in respect to the overall company objectives. This rivalry injured the competitive position of the company with respect to efficiency and costs, and often found its negative way into customer and public relations.

Since product departments are the profit centers and the focal point at which product decisions are to be made, a problem developed on how to resolve interdepartmental product-scope conflicts. A product-scope conflict is disagreement as to what products belong to which department. A newly developed product might easily fit the product areas of more than one department. Such overlapping products may look extremely promising, as potentially highly profitable, and department managers vie for the right to produce and sell them. It would seem that such conflicts are properly the jurisdiction of Division General Managers and/or Group Executives. That is usually the case, but frequently such conflicts are fought out at the department level. There is a widespread feeling that product responsibility will be assigned to the department which already has the product activity well in hand. This works well for products developed within a particular department, but fosters open warfare when a product is developed in the corporate research division. Thus "product-grabbing" occurs from time to time. Division general managers appear to have been distinctly reluctant to take action to settle product disputes within their own divisions, and even more reluctant to bring product disputes to the attention of group executives when the disputes involve a department outside of their divisions. This reluctance is not fully understood; probably some of it stems from a sincere desire to use "Management by Persuasion." When persuasiveness does not work, the problem is allowed to remain unsolved rather than to resort to stronger methods or to refer the matter to higher authority.

The practice of product-grabbing stems from the philosophy of decentralization taken to an extreme, which is the underlying belief that a department has responsibility for products which it successfully makes and sells; and that if two departments are involved in an overlapping product responsibility, favor will ultimately accrue to the department most successful in that product area. Therefore, it is better to present top management with an accomplished fact, a well-developed product, with an on-going profitable new product line, rather than bringing up questions prematurely by letting management in on the early stages of a development. Some departments in which the practice of product grabbing is the most common go to all kinds of extremes to protect the secrecy of their activities from other departments with product claims when beginning to exploit a new product possibility.[41] This was often the case between the

Hotpoint Division and the General Electric branded division producing the same types of products, before the two were combined under one division in late 1965. "Such protections have on occasion gone to the extreme of establishing a conspiracy with a customer for the purpose of maneuvering into a position of accomplished fact and thus get the jump on another competing department,"[42] says Webb. Such maneuvering of sales organizations of competing departments must have had an adverse effect on the company image and prestige with the particular customer who was the focal point of the competition.

The belief that product-grabbing may encourage healthy internal competition has not been accepted as valid by most of General Electric top management. It is not the purpose here to evaluate the company's feelings on this matter; the discussion is offered only to present how this practice affected the measurements used by the firm. Webb went on to condemn corporate practices in a paper which did *not* receive wide circulation. He said:

It is believed that product grabbing practices have seriously impeded the clear definition of product scope for departments, that the persistent belief in the practice of product grabbing on the part of some Department and Divison General Managers has given them reason to oppose and delay the clarification of product scopes; and that product grabbing stems from component selfish actions, very largely, resulting from the "one measurement" concept. The real solution lies in making very clear the relationship between over-all company interests and measurement of a department and a department manager and making this clear with respect to determinations of salaries and Incentive Compensation.[43]

From the Webb report and other sources it can be assumed that product-grabbing was a serious and widespread problem resulting from a more widely accepted view that profitability was *the* measurement and that the other seven were only secondary measurements, if in fact these seven were of any importance at all.

A second problem, noted as far back as 1957, caused by this one-measurement outlook by some managers, and also caused by older managers who gave only lip service to the new philosophy, was that dedicated managers could see a discontinuity between what the company was preaching and what was being done. The management-education program was well developed: extensive courses at Crotonville; departmental education programs; three of the four *Professional Management* books were published and well circulated, communicating the overall objectives of the company; the eight key result areas of measurement were well publicized; and the high integrity and character of the company (this is before the price-fixing scandal broke) was much discussed. Yet the younger, lower-level manager who had been weaned on this new philosophy began to see through the one-measurement concept, which developed into division or department selfishness. They wondered whether the new philosophy was hollow or whether the company (top management) really believed in it.

If it had been just a particular manager, such as a department general manager, who took these "component selfish" actions contrary to the philosophy of his own manager and group executive, it could have been written off as a failure of a particular department manager, which could have been corrected by measurement and counseling and if necessary by replacement. Unfortunately, this component selfishness in many instances seemed to be acting in complete harmony with the philosophy of his group executive. At least, this was the picture as seen by a number of present managers who have asked to be anonymous.[a]

The "One-result Area" Concept

Throughout most of the 1960s, General Electric's top management through the group and division levels placed a disproportioned emphasis on profitability. Deemphasizing the importance of the other seven key result areas was caused by errors in forecasting and legal problems which taxed the company for working capital, and hence the need for current results dominated the situation. From 1961 to 1964 General Electric paid out over one hundred million dollars in the antitrust suits. The company was looking for money to pay for the antitrust suits and continue investments and dividends. At about the same time the computer business began to drain cash at a much faster rate than anticipated. A major error in planning the computer venture might be at the base of the cash drain. General Electric planned too low on the computer business; they fell behind almost from the outset. To make money in this area you have to be Number 1, 2, or 3. IBM is Number 1; GE should have aimed for 2, but didn't. Had GE developed a specialty, e.g. computers for banks, they would have had a better chance at success. General Electric put a lot of money into this area over a long period of time, but was able to bail itself out by selling much of the hardware side of the computer business to Honeywell. GE is still in the computer field, with time-sharing services, communication equipment, and process computer business. The computer area cost a great deal of money and was never out of the red. *Dun's Review* estimates that the computer business "has bled conservatively $400 million from profits (equal to $4.44 a share before taxes per year) over the past fourteen years."[44] Philip Reed said, "This is the first one [business] I know of, of any magnitude, that we pulled out."[45]

Another capital drain was the nuclear-power business. Currently, General Electric has about 45 percent of the nuclear-power market and has invested between $150 and $350 million, and has yet to turn a profit.[46] Philip Reed said, "Chuck Rieger [currently president of Ebasco and at one time head of General Electric's Nuclear Energy Division] took on many jobs under 'estimated costs'

---

[a]In fairness to those executives who expressed this opinion in confidence, these judgments can be easily concluded as truthful and obvious from the speeches made inside the company which were attacking this problem.

and he estimated low."[47] Alvin Butkas of *Dun's Review* wrote in 1970, "it is still questionable whether General Electric will make any big money in nuclear generation before 1980."[48] Although experts now believe that GE is currently doing very well in this area, General Electric scientists had advised management as early as 1945 that it would be at least forty years before nuclear energy could be used to produce electric power commercially.[49] Nevertheless, General Electric decided to enter the field, to avoid the risk of being left out should atomic generation of electricity become feasible. As Drucker notes, General Electric entered the nuclear reactor market as a defensive measure rather than as an innovation.[50]

A third major capital drain was the jet-engine business. This venture was not so great a capital drain as the others, but some income was needed. General Electric, Rolls Royce, and Germany all developed the jet engine independently during World War II, but General Electric has had a great deal of trouble competing in the field. Some feel this has been caused by neglecting to develop new models, as Pratt & Whitney has done.[51] General Electric did invest a great deal of money in the engine for Lockheed's C-5A, the Air Force's super cargo, hoping it would be converted into a commercial airliner. Butkas claims,

The real irony of the C-5A debacle is that General Electric's financial muscle was strained to the point to where it had to bow out of the bidding for the engines on Boeing's 747, of which 197 were already either delivered or on order.[52]

Thus, through most of the 1960s General Electric had a cash problem which forced concentrating on current returns at the expense of the long term. During the 1950s, when the plans were being formulated for the sixties, a current executive recalls that the management expected these various areas to be losing money before profits were received. "But, we thought they [each cash drain area] would be staggered; they weren't and it put pressure on current results. Sure we had long-range planning going on, both at the top and in the department," he went on, "but we had to put body English on it, because we needed quick results. The bottoms-up plans got cut at the division level, to get current earnings." The implication seems to be that there is much more freedom of decision and truer decentralization during prosperous years for prosperous departments than would be the case during lean periods and less profitable departments.

Management by Objectives

In the early 1950s the eight key result areas were agreed upon and feedback mechanisms were designed to be used to control the system. "In theory," says Paul Mills, "the more that can be quantified, the sharper the measurements."[53]

Thus, results became an important word. "This, I assure you," says Mills, "produced a lot of bitching." Smiddy led the drive to think through and to organize a systematic method for evaluating the appropriateness of goals and the effectiveness of each component toward its goals. It was Smiddy who felt that one of the major education jobs of his Management Consultation Services was to teach objective setting or goal setting to the operating departments. Sectional and departmental objectives were derived from the overall divisions. Divisional objectives were derived from the overall group and company objectives. Smiddy expected that managerial effectiveness should be measured by quantitative and qualitative comparisons of actions and results against the predetermined goals.

Management by objectives, which Smiddy was advocating before Drucker popularized the philosophy in his 1954 *Practice of Management*, can be found in the literature much before 1950. Yet students of business policy formulation of today are quick to point out that "management by objectives" practiced in the 1920s and 1930s is not the same as "management by objectives" practiced today and that which was advocated by Smiddy and by Drucker, as a consultant to Smiddy, as early as 1951.[54] Business policy formulation between the two world wars was basically short-term planning, with the major task of managers, including the chief executive, to plan the adaptation of the organization to the changing conditions. Henri Fayol attributed much of his success as a manager to this type of planning which was based on the "General Survey."[55] The "General Survey" consisted of sizing up the situation in the economy and industry with respect to: the competitive situation; the financial and operating picture; analyses of sales, production, costs, executive organization, etc. The sizing up was followed by recommendations for action. Such general surveys were conducted when management was faced with major problems. A pioneer consultant, James O. McKinsey, followed this method of "management by objectives," although he didn't use the term.[56] Adaptation to changing conditions was the method of teaching business policy formulation at such leading institutions as Harvard. Melvin T. Copeland's landmark article on the subject published in 1940 stresses this concept.[57] Thus, this short-term method of planning was, in fact, practiced by big business, including General Electric. The method of setting objectives was then to decide on a course of action in the light of the situation facing the company at a particular time. Immediate profits and adaptability to meet changing current conditions were of prime importance, and were therefore the measurements used to evaluate the past managerial decisions. Cornell Professor of Business Policy Frank Gilmore says, "There was seldom a clear concept of objectives or long-range plans to which management was committed. . . . Major planning was initiated only when management sensed that a serious policy problem existed."[58]

At General Electric in the early 1950s it was felt that this type of business planning was unacceptable. Sporadic diagnosis was replaced by constant surveillance. Continuous planning was part of each component and Harold Smiddy informally saw that it was performed. Two years after Smiddy retired, John B. McKitterick was made Manager of Corporate Planning Operation, which was a special corporate section. In 1965 McKitterick was elevated to Vice President and his corporate planning was given full-fledged status as a Services component. The change from sporadic diagnosis to continuous reappraisal of corporate policy has been in keeping with Peter Drucker's advice of the early 1950s. General Electric's attention had been focused more on the seizing of opportunities than on the solution of problems.[59]

Mills explains that management by objectives best describes the General Electric system, and one aspect of this system is the measuring stage. If the measuring stage is properly "implemented," he says, "it can go a long way in allowing managers to keep their 'mitts' on the organization."[60] But Mills reflects, "A lot of measurement work was given to clerk types who mechanically grind out comparison of the planned versus the output, without explanations of why."[61] What he means by "without explanations" is that the "clerk types," who work up comparisons of the planned work against what actually happened, do not explain the variances, when found, nor do they explain why the planned and actual results matched when the environment changed to make this result unnatural. Without the explanations, he says, "Variances are meaningless."[62] When you have management by objectives, you expect control by exception. But Mills notes, "Control by exception is spoken about, but what the financial people are doing at General Electric, is managing by patterns. If something doesn't fit a pattern, it pops out."[63] As a long-time manager in the financial area, Paul Mills adds that even when patterns look good to the financial analysts you "may have a pattern which could run you to bankruptcy."[64] This may happen when patterns become so dominant for decision purposes that management becomes blind to the objectives it has set for itself.

Mills spent his last three years outside GE as a manager in the highly dynamic chemical industry. He had the right to spend up to a quarter of a million dollars if he wanted.[65] He says,

I couldn't get figures which estimated the percent of project completion versus real completion. I couldn't get what was done ahead of schedule. When you don't know what work is completed ahead of schedule, you may look at your financial statement and think you are overspending.[66]

Unhappily, he protests,

Most budgets aren't worth a damn as control documents. Budgets are made five, six, eighteen months ahead of the period to be controlled. In the chemical industry, the dynamic picture can change overnight, so a budget is not worth much as control.[67]

Turning to the construction field, in which Mills was Vice President of Ebasco Industries, Inc., he said that he tried to use an eighteen-month rolling forward total:

So that I was looking ahead of the average time [18 months] it took from receipt of orders to the time we could put the average plant on stream; here budgets for control are for the birds. I tried min-max budgets; I've tried them all. One thing for sure, a fixed budget is almost worthless in many industries.[68]

He included in the meaning of that last sentence much of the electrical and chemical industries.

The belief that profitability was *the* most important measurement of a man's ability, and the desire to protect oneself, as evidenced by product-grabbing, created a need to find measurements which would encourage managers to concentrate on the goals and objectives of the total organization. The next chapter will discuss this problem.

Conclusion

The sweeping organization changes of the early 1950s produced shocks felt strongly until about 1960; then the firm experienced new shocks caused by managerial errors in forecasting. General Electric management thought of decentralizing as far back as the 1930s. Former President Charles E. Wilson relates:

My own design and desire, as early as 1930, was decentralization but by the time I became President in 1940 we were on the verge of a world war. . . . When I returned from my duties with the War Production Board in late 1944 I had full realization of the tremendous changes the war had brought about and spent my remaining years as President capitalizing on my belief in the potentials. . . . By 1949 I knew we finally had to decentralize, and hence, the efforts of Mr. Cordiner.[69]

These past few chapters have offered a history of the organization changes, the philosophy behind the moves, and, it is hoped, some flavor of the organization.

Evaluation of the Individual Under Decentralization

One of the major problems found in management, whether it is centralized or decentralized, is how to appraise the collective performance of a group, division, or department; or the performance of the individual who heads the unit. It is conceivable that the executive's performance might be good even though his department has results that are considered poor, or vice versa. The overall determinant of departmental performance on occasion is based on one criterion, return on investment, and both the departmental performance and its top executive are judged in terms of this criterion. At the Columbia University Roundtables on Management (1954) an alternate approach was discussed.[1] Instead of judging the executive by the results of his department alone, emphasis would be on how he does his work—on his ability to size up competition, to think, to spot and correct weak areas, to work with his people, and so forth. This type of measurement is difficult to apply, but it is pertinent.[2]

Measurements

At the Columbia University Roundtables, one member presented a comprehensive list of criteria for measuring managers. The list was the eight key result areas used by the General Electric Company as presented in Chapter 4—Profitability, Market Position, Productivity, Product Leadership, Personnel Development, Employee Attitudes, Public Responsibility, and Balance Between Short-Range and Long-Range Goals. It can be assumed Harold Smiddy presented this list to the conference, since he was one of the many distinguished participants, which also included Peter Drucker, who helped form the measurement concept, Wallace Sayre (CCNY), and William Newman (Columbia), the only academic participants among the twenty conference attendants, most of whom were top business executives and business consultants. After the General Electric list of eight key result areas was presented, William Newman reported,

The list was recognized as needing further definition of sub-factors, adaption to specified operations, and other refinements. Nevertheless, it does provide comprehensive coverage within a manageable number of factors.[3]

Further discussion brought out a number of areas needing refinement or reevaluation, the same problems with which General Electric managers have wrestled over the past seventeen years. It was noted that along with this multiple-factor approach to management appraisal for control purposes was the need to vary the weights of the various areas according to a particular situation. The product research which affects profitability and product leadership must be given much more weight in a department producing computers than one producing electric tape, where the growth prospects are much more modest. This problem falls under the eighth key result area—balance of long- and short-range goals—and it still is a most difficult problem to solve in practice.

In planning the eighth key result area a most subjective factor is how to assign weights to the factors considered important by top management. Since each operating department produces different products, each at different stages of product life and each somewhat unique, it holds that each product will require emphasis to be placed on different factors with different weights. "Tomorrow's breadwinners," to use a Drucker expression,[4] would require planning emphasis looking toward the long run, while "today's or yesterday's breadwinners" require a control measurement to reflect today's cost and contribution to profit. Thus, while it is most difficult to compose the quantitative and qualitative measurements in the first seven key result areas, the subjectivity of the eighth area almost negates any comparison of products. What the key result areas can help do is to measure past performance against expected results. This type of organized measurement allows better use of management by objectives, but it does not make management by objectives any less subjective. There is a danger that if the subjectivity of the eighth key result area is not appreciated and managers improperly read more objectivity into the measurements than exists, this approach will be reduced to a formula. It is doubtful with the state of the art that any formula could be flexible enough to reflect what has happened, to properly measure the management, and to fit all situations and products. Subjective judgments involved in such measurements used for control purposes open the way for clashes of opinion between top management and operating executives.

A cursory look at the eight key result areas in GE gives the impression that a series of detailed operating standards are used to appraise departmental performance and also executive achievement. But once the subjectivity of the standards is understood then it can be readily seen that the eight key result areas when used to evaluate the departmental executive actually emphasize "how he does his work," e.g., how does he size up his product and competition? how does he think? how energetic is he in correcting weak spots? how does he treat his men? how does he plan? and so forth. Since the measurements are subjective and there is no one best way of managing, these measures are most difficult to apply as a control device. The more objective the evaluation superiors believe the measurement criteria to be, the more these measurements become a method of domination by the superior. That is, they become strict standards needing little interpretation, and thereby become control devices in a negative sense.

Control can have two meanings in management. The positive meaning for "control" is the ability to direct oneself and one's work. The negative meaning is domination of one person by another. With management by objectives being the central theme in General Electric's philosophy of control, the negative meaning of the word has no place; where the control becomes domination of one by another, there is a breakdown between corporate philosophy and corporate reality. Drucker notes, "One of the major contributions of management by objectives is that it enables us to substitute management by self-control for management by domination."[5] Because of the possible negative connotation of the word "control," Smiddy dropped its use to describe a function of management in favor of "measuring" at the time he introduced Hopf's elements of the leadership function into the corporate professional management blue books.

The concept of self-control is certainly not new with General Electric; it is plainly found in the writings of Follett, L. Gilbreth, Hopf, and others. It underlies the managing philosophy of "pushing decisions down to the lowest possible level." Self-control requires a manager to know what his goals are and to be able to measure his performance against the goals. It does not require exact quantitative measurements, but it does require relevant and simple measurements—relevant in that the efforts are directed toward the correct goals or objectives; simple so that they are understandable to the manager in question.

Drucker adds:

Each manager should have the information he needs to measure his own performance and should receive it soon enough to make any changes necessary for the desired results. And this information should go to the manager himself, and not to his superior. It should be a means of self-control, not a tool of control from above. . . .

General Electric has a special service—the traveling auditors. The auditors study every one of the managerial units of the company thoroughly at least once a year. But their report goes to the manager of the unit studied. There can be little doubt that the feeling of confidence and trust in the company that even casual contact with General Electric managers reveals, is directly traceable to this practice of using information for self-control rather than for control from above.[6]

Drucker's statement does seem to conflict with the previously reported "financial fraternity" concept. The fact that the traveling auditors send the report to the manager of the unit studied does not prevent informal information passing to other members of the so-called "fraternity." The real conflict between Drucker and the fraternity concept lies in "the feeling of confidence and trust" found by Drucker. Evidently, various people have perceived the situation differently. It should be noted that Paul Mills, who was cited earlier in the discussion of the concept, spent about thirty years as a GE employee, some of that time in finance. Drucker, as an outside consultant, was very involved with

GE for about five years, when he was assisting Smiddy in the reorganization in the early 1950s.

The foregoing discussion does not imply that reports are not sent to top management, those above the manager being measured, for they are and should be. Successful managers, those who have made it to the top levels of organization, have normally received their promotions because they initiated work, they got things done and done right. Although they talk delegation, and perhaps even believe they practice it, truly letting go of the reins is difficult for men who have been so successful by being action-oriented production managers of operations close to the movement of products. Creating the proper climate for decentralization to work is extremely difficult. The need to know what is being done below is strong. The urge to meddle in the affairs of subordinates once a manager receives information about his subordinates is sometimes overwhelming, and all the philosophy to the contrary will not alter what may occur in practice. But with properly trained leaders, a greater percent will overcome the strong desire to "take charge" and entrust subordinates with full responsibility for certain assignments if they know what is happening and that the risk entailed by failure on the part of the subordinate is not excessive. Raymond Villers concludes that:

The high-ranking executive who is responsible for the operations of large sections of an industrial organization and who is not in a position to make use of effective controls, tends to be tyrannical because he is worried. He will give much greater independence to his subordinates if he knows that their mistakes will be detected before any irreparable damage results.[7]

The evaluation of workers is closely tied to the controls used to assure that the organization is continuing along a proper path. The eight key result areas are categories of measurements used to ascertain the relative position of a product department. Some of the measurements quantify particular aspects of the job performed by a product department; most compare one aspect of the department against predetermined standards. Some measurements are quantifiable and objective; others are less easily visualized and are very subjective. Measuring nonproduct department managers is very difficult and presents a problem which the company philosophy has yet to solve. Even evaluating or measuring a whole division is difficult, especially a Services division. Before you can really control an organization, you must be able to evaluate and measure it by objective and/or subjective means. Some of the objectives and goals for service organizations and managers have fruition periods of fifteen to twenty years. Measures made of the effectiveness of an initial decision might be easily designed, but the manager initiating the course of action has usually either retired or been promoted. Lemuel Boulware, retired Vice President of Employee Relations at General Electric, believes that evaluation and the measuring of managers is "the toughest problem in business management—at every level and whether in operations or services."[8] Even when figures are available for evaluation of product department managers, the subjective evaluation still commands the central position in the evaluation. It is only the product department manager who heads a profit center; all other managers are either above, below, or outside (such as in services divisions) the company's profit centers. So it is only the product department managers who can be measured by the eight key result areas, and there are fewer than two hundred of these managers in the company. But even if much quantitative information is available on a manager's work, the subjective evaluation still determines the overall appraisal of the manager. Boulware says:

When sitting in judgment on a manager for bonus or promotion purposes . . . the quantitative information available does not show the causes behind the figures. The qualitative enters as the finally determining factor most every time. How much of the manager's "results," as shown in the figures, was due to the way he drew on his own inner resources, and how much was due to factors beyond his control such as a surge in the industry market or a mistake or strike suffered by a competitor? Was an advantage in volume temporary, and could competitors be expected to . . . get back their share?[9]

Measuring Services

The task of measuring the performance of Services components and their managers is even more difficult than judging decentralized operating managers and their components. The output of Services is largely intangible, which leads to difficulties in comparing costs with results.

General Electric's philosophy is based on management by objectives. Thus, Services are measured and controlled by the setting of an evaluation of progress toward objectives. These objectives are set once a year, at the time the budget is established. The objectives are reviewed by members of the Executive Office— that is, by all the Services officers together with the Operating Group Executives. One past executive called it "our day in court" when the budget and objectives were presented. He said:

We would go down through the objectives specifically and explain what Management Consultation Services, let's say, was going to do for each one of the other components, and in this meeting agreement was made on how much money would be budgeted for each objective. Such things as writing the philosophy books, what we were going to do to management development, plans for the Crotonville school, what organizations we were going to look at, why and how, and so forth, were discussed in specific detail.[10]

Measuring Services is very subjective. The Chief Executive Officer meets with the executive office once a year for the executive review of budgets and objectives. This executive review should not be confused with the business review, which is a review of each operating department made twice a year.[11] Although this formal executive review occurs once a year, there are numerous monthly progress reports from each Services and Group to the Executive Office. These monthly reports state what each component is doing against what was planned at the beginning of the budgeting period. Objectives can change during the year based upon the need, but always with prior agreement. The Chief Executive Officer, sitting above the Services Vice President, is able to judge from the reaction of the other corporate executives as to what and how each Services is doing and if any changes are warranted.

A difficulty in measuring Services is that frequently Services projects would not have results forthcoming for about twenty years. It must be remembered that at General Electric the word "Services" covers a wide range of activities; some are short termed, some long termed, and some activities are more closely associated with operating work than the traditional concept of staff work. For example, one Services activity at General Electric that is closely associated with operating work is union negotiations. This type of work is not looking twenty years ahead; it's taking care of today's needs. In this case, the New York office directs all the bargaining. The General Engineering Laboratory, where General Electric has designated capital for research, is in a sense doing operating work. When Engineering Services is "training" engineering people for operating work, that really is not Services work as much as it is operating work on a pooled basis. This would be easier to measure than when one is dealing with the pure Services function, such as what is going to happen sixteen to twenty years in the future. In that case, the measurement must be subjective and it must be on "how is a manager doing today in getting operating people ready for tomorrow."[12] Measuring Services is not unlike the evaluation of skating, diving, and gymnastics, in that all judgments, even for the "expert," are subjective. But in athletics the event is evaluated as it occurs; in Services the evaluation takes place long before results from actions are expected.

Most of the personnel in Services have been promoted out of Operations. It should be understood that the establishment of the Services organization came as part of the 1951 reorganization, and it was at this time that Cordiner and Smiddy decided that Services people would get their reputation and strength based on an "authority of knowledge." Therefore, Smiddy scoured the various line departments for highly authoritative people to be put into Services. In order to attract them the company had to give them higher salaries than they were earning, and many of these people were the highest-paid men within the Operating departments. Smiddy felt that the line people would come to Services for guidance because of their tremendous reputations as successful operating people, and these were the types that were attracted to Services work and were highly successful. One problem was evident, even at the early stages—that the Services expert often felt the time spent on long-range planning less tangible and more frustrating because, as Arthur Vinson, retired Executive Vice President, noted,

There are no quickly obtainable evaluations of progress . . . he feels at first as though he is not earning his pay; that he is unable to get his teeth into the problem; that the work that others [line people] are doing is more important.[13]

Another problem somewhat related to control of Services personnel, which was not handled by the philosophy or the practice of the company, is how to handle Services personnel after they lose some of their "authority of knowledge." While the managers who had been promoted into Services were searching for and teaching better methods of work, some of the line people began to have even greater knowledge than their Services advisors, through their own advancements within Operations and being right on the firing line. In the mid-1950s Smiddy and Cordiner discovered a tremendous problem, because Services work had always been considered of higher status and higher compensation than Operating work, as noted in Chapter 3. It became necessary to send Services people back into Operations. Through time some Services people lost some "authority of knowledge" to Operating people, and Smiddy concluded that these men must go back into Operations—but they had to keep their higher Services salary, because they were not being reprimanded for poor work; they were going back for a "refresher course" in Operations, with the expectation that they would soon return to Services. Unfortunately, the higher salary commanded by the shifted Services people wasn't in the structure—the pay scale of Operations would not accept such high salaries, and the fairness of these high salaries compared to the salaries of Operating men who did not have a Services background doing the same work is questionable. This posed a tremendous problem for Cordiner and for the salary evaluation group in the Compensation Service, which was under Lemuel Boulware for the decade of the 1950s. William Greenwood says:

To my knowledge, I don't remember any who made the complete switch from line to Services to line and back to Services. Several were sent back for the so-called "refresher courses" but they became so ingrained with their first love, Operations, that they themselves didn't want to come back into the very difficult kind of Services work where measurements were so subjective and so difficult to understand. They obtained greater pleasure in seeing things go out the door than they did in looking at research studies and thinking through corporate philosophy.
    As a result of all this, I feel that Services today possibly are weaker than they were in the 1950's and that something will have to be done to get people to come into Services out of the line and to stay in Services using "refresher courses" on the basis of a loan or something like that to various Operating Divisions. I don't think this has been done since the new structure was inaugurated in 1951. One opinion, reinforced many times, still remains, the best

Services people are those who have had on the line experience in rough managerial situations.[14]

Lemuel Boulware, however, known for his "hard" approach to union relations, and the 1958 recipient of the SAM human relations award, does not think the qualitative measurements used for Services organizations make for any more formidable a problem than measurements for Operations.

In operations there is a presumed luxury of positive figures on volume, profit, percentage of profit to sales, return on investment, inventory turnover, market performance, and percentage of the industry's actual sales. But this quantitative information frequently is as inaccurate as [subjective] judgments. When profits are substantially overstated because of inflation and when allowable depreciation is far too little for replacement in kind, this quantitative information without careful restructuring can be and often is basically inadequate. Even if accurate, it is very misleading if taken by itself.[15]

In *The Truth About Boulwarism,*[16] he spells out very plainly the requirements of his Employee and Plant Community Relations Services Division. All nine departments under Boulware were engaged in persuading operating personnel in some aspect of work. And he frankly admits that the determining factor in the success of this effort at persuasion (without authority) was the degree to which each operating manager right up to the top made it clear to his subordinates that they were being measured for reward or even survival either by how they embraced and effectively carried out these top-management-approved recommendations or by how successful they were in achieving better results by alternate means of their own devising toward the same ends. Boulware said recently:

The big problem was to get operating people at each level to recognize the need to make room for new work added besides the old "metal cutting and paper shuffling," and to become both sufficiently competent and sufficiently active in that work. This work did not come to them automatically as in the case of operating duties. Rather it was an investment ahead of time in "prior homework" that would yield increased cooperation and productivity constantly as well as providing insurance against periodic disasters.

Because of our being constantly in the field, it was not hard to observe who was going at which parts of our program in earnest. This was a sure clue both for our discussions with superior operating authority as to further pressure by them on which of their subordinates, and for my own judgments as to which of my specialized departments were being acceptably persuasive.[17]

Boulware admits that the control function is complicated in Services by the fact that the Services have to engage in a very sizeable and unpredictable amount of "fire fighting work in addition to meeting ... [the] main responsibility for fire prevention."[18]

The eight key result areas are used to measure the approximately two hundred departments in General Electric. But Services and, on the Operating side, the levels of Division and Group are not measured or controlled by the eight key result areas. These top-level managers are measured very differently. The philosophy of the company concentrates on the profit centers—the departments. The Measurements Project, which has yet to complete its almost twenty-year search for operational measurements at the department level, has done almost nothing to develop organized thinking on measurements in other areas. The measurements study team has stated that they can consider how to approach the problem of formulating functional measurements only after the operational measurements have been substantially completed, and that further development on the measurement of the work of a manager (at all levels) is contingent upon the measurements developed in the operational and functional areas.[19] Therefore, the philosophy of the firm in this most important control area has yet to be organized and unified. When asked, "How do you evaluate the Group Vice Presidents reporting to you?" Vice Chairman Jack S. Parker began by saying, "We [the Corporate Executive Office] all have our own method and we each are looking for different things."[20]

Measuring the work of a manager is difficult. The type of measurement used, that is, what is looked at or considered to be important, may vary with each level of the hierarchy. This is not to imply (as may or may not be the case) that leadership and management are not fundamentally the same at all levels. It is saying that the information received and methods of measuring the effectiveness of a particular manager may be altered with the level of the hierarchy and with the particular job performed. At lower levels more quantifiable measurements may be found. A marketing manager responsible for sales, for example, could be evaluated using such yardsticks as actual sales to quotas; accounts received over sixty days, over ninety days; expenses versus budget; etc.[21] As we ascend the hierarchy other measures must be considered. Professor Ronald B. Shuman notes, "Broadly speaking, the higher the hierarchy of command, the less factually measurable the accomplishments of the manager."[22] In *The Management of Men*, Shuman notes,

The quality of top-level management varies over a wide range and is not easily measurable by objective standards. . . . Proper selection of executives . . . is severely hampered by lack of quantitative measurements for the more important but intangible of human qualities.[23]

Drucker seconds this thought by saying that managing is a process and

No matter how much we can quantify, the basic phenomena are qualitative ones: change and innovation, risk and judgment, growth and decay, dedication, vision, rewards, and motivation.[24]

It seems that management is searching for a method to measure and control other managers, particuarly at what may be termed the "command level." The measuring of Services managers and of managers above the department level in the line, i.e., division and group, is most difficult and highly subjective. Some hope for a method of measuring these managers the same way, with the same validity used to quantitatively measure the manual worker. This is, in the state of the art, a vain hope indeed. Those raised in the scientific management school can plainly see and measure what constitutes "productivity" for the manual worker. But Services people are not manual workers; they are knowledge workers. Drucker has correctly noted, "Knowledge work is not easily defined in quantitative terms, and may indeed be incapable of quantification altogether."[25] Frederick W. Taylor asked what constitutes "productivity" for the manual worker. He never asked the same question for the industrial engineer, the man who was applying his "scientific management."[26] Productivity for the knowledge worker is not as yet definable, and therefore must be measured primarily on subjective qualities.

Measuring Services seems to be a most difficult process—much more thought is needed in order to develop measurements that will be effective in establishing the achievements made in working on the right problem of the organization. Because measuring Services is difficult, it should not be implied that measuring the individual manager or individual contributor in the line is any less difficult. The next area of this chapter discusses this aspect of the appraising problem at General Electric.

Appraising the Individual

Appraising the individual contributor or manager is an integral part of the measuring or control function. Appraisal of employees has different goals in different organizations. In General Electric the purpose of appraisals is to aid the individual to become better in his position, to develop and aid in his self-development, and not to determine whether or not he should get a raise. This is a very significant part of how General Electric proposes that managers be measured effectively. The appraisal plan in General Electric, which was initiated about 1953, required that at least once a year a man write down what is required in his position in a self-development book. In a duplicate book his boss would write down what he thought was required in that position. The reason that the "job duties," "job requirements," or "job scope" was written down each year by both the incumbent and his supervisor is that, as Norman F. Maier has pointed out,

Until the two agree on the . . . job areas there is bound to be disagreement in appraising or rating performance. The use of job descriptions and previous experience of the superior on the subordinate's job does not remove the discrepancy.[27]

Each incumbent then would rate himself against what was required, that is on each one of the so-called functions of the position. The superior would do the same thing. Later they would exchange books, discuss the differences, and come to an agreement. The differences may be that the incumbent of a position failed to work on one of the "functions," but that did not mean he was a failure; rather, it may have been with the full knowledge of the boss because of the urgency of some of the other factors of the position. This is a justifiable reason why a particular part of a function had not been fulfilled. A new incumbent in a position might be at a variance with his manager in what is required of a position after the first year—position guides are fairly comprehensive, but even a six- to thirteen-page position guide cannot and should not detail a job into a strait jacket. However, it should define the scope and purpose of the position adequately. The second, third, and fourth years should find the incumbent and boss quite close in their evaluation of the factors of the position, unless the position has changed. In terms of recording the requirements of the position, the first part of the appraisal could have been quite repetitious, since each year both the manager and the man retain their books.

The appraisal continues with recording how the incumbent performed with respect to other factors than his specific function targets. For example, how did a manager do with planning for his component? how did he do with the organization of it? how did he do with the measurement of it? how did he do with promoting teamwork or integration? Each one of these aspects is sub-divided. Then there was a summary with respect to each category. Both the incumbent and his superior had to determine and record the strengths and weaknesses of the incumbent. The formal writing of the report in terms of strengths and weaknesses was important, so that a person was able to capitalize on his strengths and could either aid himself by concentrating in the future on his weaknesses or seeking to avoid them.

Another part of the appraisal deals with whether the individual feels that his present line of work is the kind of work he should be in permanently, or for how long. If he decides that this is not to be his permanent kind of work, then what steps should he take in order to get himself into the kind of position where he thinks he would be better qualified, or which he would like better? The superior has to record for future reference what he as a manager would do to aid that individual get out of that position, for if the individual were still in the same position a year or two later, these statements might not only become very embarrassing to the supervisor but might also be spotlighting a problem.

Each one of the appraisal books written by the incumbent and his superior was not only a performance and development review, but the comments pertinent to each were signed and sent to the second-level boss above, so that he would sign and take note of the appraisal. This, then, became a permanent record, not in the company files, but rather among the three people—the incumbent of the position, his manager, and his manager's manager. These books are returned to the employee when he leaves the company, because the sole purpose of these appraisals is to make a person a better manager or individual contributor.[28]

William Greenwood remembers:

The appraisal was done quite religiously from 1954 to 1958, after that I really don't know [he left General Electric]. I don't know how widespread that procedure was except that I do know that Cordiner reviewed each one of the people reporting to him in this way. And I do know that he demanded that they in turn do the same thing with their incumbents because he, Cordiner, had to sign those books. As to how far down the line it really went—it was supposed to go down to the lowest level of managing—I don't know.[29]

Jack S. Parker implied that he did not adhere strictly to the above appraisal plan. He spends much effort in evaluating the group executives reporting to him. This does not mean he does not also appraise them. In evaluating these group vice presidents, Parker says he first looks at the executive himself in terms of "what is this fellow worth to the General Electric Company and how do we feel about him as an officer of the Company." He says, "If I have any doubts here, I ask what strengths would I look for in a replacement."[30] The second area Parker evaluates is the contribution of the incumbent to his operations. There he claims to look toward the future contributions and the present trade-offs between long-range and short-range contributions which the incumbent has programmed. Third, he looks to see how the customer likes the way this man is managing. He says, "I check that independently, myself."[31] And last, Parker evaluates the personnel under the executive "to see to it that better men are coming along—that is a matter of personnel and it means the future of the organization."[32] What Parker is subjectively doing is evaluating the executive in terms of what he thinks the man is worth and will be worth to the organization in four areas—company, component, customer, and personnel development. This evaluation is formalized in a report once a year to the Executive Office as a whole, of which Parker is a part. (The above is a subjective evaluation or appraisal; it should not be confused with the reports issued measuring progress against budgets, which are issued monthly.)

Lemuel Boulware explains why it is so difficult to appraise managers and knowledge workers. He believes luck and intangible factors play important roles. He says years of experience

would indicate some intangible is the determining factor in one manager having a high percentage of decisions that prove to have been good ones, while another manager of apparently equal ability and access to information would have a lower percentage.[33]

Boulware has stated:

My opinion has always been that the extra performance [of one individual over another] was not due to any superior instinct or intuition but rather to some unsensed combination of such factors as greater diligence, extra concentration, keener observation, a longer or more pertinent experience on which to draw even unknowingly, paying special attention to those facts and recommendations which have proved more likely to be trustworthy, a disciplined tough-mindedness about one's own wishful thinking, and/or some other such positive ingredient whether consciously or subconsciously injected.[34]

Smiddy insisted that "management by objectives," which centered on the assessment of performance by comparison against predetermined goals, must be practiced. The often negative attitude which Douglas McGregor developed toward many managerial practices was not aimed at this type of management. He wrote that "management by objectives" offered "an unusually promising framework within which we seek a solution [to human problems of industry]."[35] McGregor cited General Electric as one company exploring different methods of appraisal based on the assumptions of Drucker's philosophy.

At the time McGregor was complimenting General Electric on its methods of appraisal, and about eight years after Cordiner had begun decentralization, Donald Webb wrote of General Electric's performance appraisals, "There is strong evidence that many Division General Managers have never carried out effective discussions with their Department General Managers in this area and it is believed that this resistance exists at all layers."[36] Webb went on to claim that in his seventeen years' experience with the company he had never had a discussion with any of his superiors which carried out "the spirit of the new management philosophy."[37] Dr. Herbert Meyer, Consultant in Behavioral Research Service, who has studied performance appraisals for the company and has been eighteen years in a department which requires performance appraisals, claims to have had only two in all that time.[38] The philosophy referred to by both Donald Webb and Herbert Meyer is found in the *Professional Management* series dating back to 1954:

An individual who is not performing up to expectations in a particular position should be told so frankly and kindly by his manager. The individual himself should know sooner than anyone else if he is not performing up to the standards he has set for himself, or up to the requirements of the job which he has undertaken. He should be given all possible encouragement and guidance if he is trying realistically to improve his own abilities and to stretch himself toward adequate performance. He should be removed from the position if, after a fair trial and after receiving help and encouragement, he continues to fall short of expected accomplishment.[39]

McGregor suggests that there may be a sound foundation behind the widespread reluctance of managers to conduct such discussions with their employees, and that this might be tied in with the manager's reluctance to "play God." He argues that the "management by objectives" approach lessens the burdens of "playing God."[40] The question is not so much "playing God," but one of leading and managing. A good manager must of necessity "play God" in choosing people for promotion, in giving assignments to people, and in making many other choices. The problem is, can the manager do this face to face with the employee, or only behind the employee's back? In terms of management by objectives, it must be done face to face.

The main thrust of the General Electric philosophy is contained in this tenet: "Individuals . . . are motivated principally by . . . inner drives rather than by someone else's directions."[41] It is based on the contention that the company and the supervisor must set up a work situation which enables an individual to motivate himself. It is not a new philosophy, nor is it claimed to be, for it is shared by McGregor, Mayo, Hopf, Follett, and all of the human-relations philosophers. As Robert Townsend points out, "You can't motivate people. The door is locked from the inside. You can create a climate in which most of your people will motivate themselves to help the company reach its objectives."[42] The foundation for this belief is the premise that employees do not need to be controlled or commanded if they know clearly what is to be done, why it is to be done, how they are to be measured and paid, and what their advancement opportunities may be. The General Electric philosophy says,

This is the way in which strong inner urges and individual self-motivation, self-direction, self-adjustment, self-education, self-development, self-discipline, self-control, and the desire for self-realization are geared to the business enterprise.[43]

It is the company's philosophy that a healthy managerial attitude encompasses a willingness to submit to unifying direction and to work in a spirit of cooperative concern for the work of others, while at the same time seeking personal achievement and recognition. A decentralized manager must be free to cope with such problems as maintaining or improving the competitive position of the product line by improving profits without unbalancing pressures from above. The desired atmosphere was suggested by Dr. Harry Hopf:

Practically every act of management requires for its consummation that cooperative relationships be maintained between two or more persons. . . . The problem is to determine the best method of bringing about these relationships. . . . The existence of cooperation depends primarily upon the setting by top executives of an example which may be found worthy of emulation by other members of the organization.

The acid test of the existence of true cooperation is the presence of a two-fold relationship of loyalty-loyalty to his superior on the part of the subordinate and loyalty to his subordinate on the part of the superior. If this relation of mutual confidence exists, the result, in practical terms, spells the finest type of cooperation.[44]

According to Mary Parker Follett, this desired managerial attitude involves "participation," which is obtained

by an organization which provides for it, by a daily management which recognizes and acts on the principle of particpation, and by a method of settling differences, or a method of dealing with the diverse contributions of men very different in temperament, training, and attainments.[45]

For a man to develop he must be able to measure himself. Most individuals want to know how his self-evaluation compares against the evaluations of others, especially against those in power positions in relation to his own position. As part of the esteem need, people want to know that others respect and appreciate them. Appraisal by a superior may fulfill this need. Appraisal by superiors will also help direct the activities of subordinates so that they fit the needs of the superior and team and thus allow the subordinate to work in areas which will enable him to be more productive to the organization and receive higher appraisals. Ray E. Brown points out,

Criticism is hard to take, but people do want to know where they stand. Nobody likes to play a game and not know the score. . . . If the administrator is to get improvement rather than antagonism, he must be able to demonstrate disapproval without demonstrating hostility, and to do this he must be able to reserve a sufficient margin of personal detachment to permit him to be emotionally casual in expressing disapproval.[46]

People want to know how well they are doing as perceived by others. But, of course, they want to be judged "on the facts." The company philosophy has been taken directly from Peter Drucker:

Appraisals must be based on performance. Appraisal is judgment and judgment always requires a definite standard. To judge means to apply a set of values; and value judgments without clear, sharp and public standards are irrational and arbitrary. They corrupt alike the judge and judged. No matter how "scientific," no matter even how many insights it produces, an appraisal that focuses on "potential," on "personality," on "promise"—on anything that is not proven and provable performance—is an abuse.[47]

Norman Maier has conducted some pertinent research which offers evidence that appraisal interviewing (which General Electric did before the new philosophy and is now only one part of the new program) and motivating behavior are in conflict. Maier found that an appraiser is almost certain to be led into a behavior pattern which leads to some deteriorating of human relations. His studies indicate that objectives, methods, and skills are interrelated to an extent which precludes analysis of any one aspect separately. Maier suggests that the appraisal interview be replaced by an interview concerned with employee development. If ratings are required for other purposes, he contends that they should be delayed until after the interview and that less emphasis be placed on the fault-finding technique.

During the 1960s General Electric made extensive progress in this area, as suggested by Maier. A small group known as Behavioral Research Service became responsible for company leadership in this area. Experiments conducted within the company by Dr. Herbert H. Meyer[48] helped to formulate a new method of appraisal reviews. Meyer studied the traditional annual performance appraisal method by testing it against a new method referred to as Work Planning and Review (WP and R). Studies had been made, and are currently being conducted, on how much and what kinds of employee participation would be most useful, and under what conditions. That is, what type and how much "participative" management is needed. Meyer worked with Dr. Emanuel Kay, a Research Specialist in General Electric's Behavioral Research Service, and Dr. John R.P. French, Jr., Program Director at the Research Center for Group Dynamics Institute for Social Research, University of Michigan. They were able to develop the following conclusions:

1. Criticism has a negative effect on achievement. ("The subordinate reacted defensively about 54% of the time when criticized.")

2. Praise has little effect one way or the other. ("Evidence we gathered indicated clearly that praise tended to have no effect, perhaps because it was regarded as the sandwich which surrounded the raw meat of criticism.")

3. A tendency for a subordinate to overrate his own performance ("only two of the ninety-two participants estimated their performance to be below the average point on the scale") was reduced by the appraisal process ("over 80% of the participants saw their manager's evaluation as being less favorable than self-estimates").

4. Performance improves most when specific goals are established. ("The average percent accomplishment estimate for those performance items that *did* get translated into goals was 65, while the percent accomplishment goals estimate for those items that *did not* get translated into goals was about 27!")

5. Critical appraisal produces inferior performance. ("Improvement in the most-criticized aspects of performance was considerably less than improvements realized in other areas.")

6. Participation by the employee in the goal-setting procedure helps produce favorable results, providing the employee normally worked under high participative levels.

7. Separate appraisals should be held for different purposes. ("It is unrealistic

to expect a single performance appraisal program to achieve every conceivable need. It seems foolish to have a manager serving in the self-conflicting role as a counselor helping a man to improve his performance when at the same time, he is presiding as a judge over the same employee's salary action case.")[49]

The company's experience suggests that Work Planning and Review:

are strictly man-to-man in character, rather than having a father-and-son flavor, as did so many of the traditional performance appraisals. This seems to be due to the fact that it is much more natural under the W P & R program for the subordinate to take the initative when performance on past goals is being reviewed. Thus, in listening to the subordinate's review of performance, problems, and failings, the manager is automatically cast in the role of *counselor*. This role for the manager, in turn, results naturally in a problem-solving discussion.

In the traditional performance appraisal interview, on the other hand, the manager is automatically cast in the role of *judge*. The subordinate's natural reaction is to assume a defensive posture, and thus all the necessary ingredients for an argument are present. . . .

In general, the W P & R approach appears to be a better way of defining what is expected of an individual and how he is doing on the job. Whereas the traditional performance appraisal often results in resistance to the manager's attempts to help the subordinate, the W P & R approach brings about acceptance of such attempts.[50]

Because of the research by Meyer, Kay, and French in 1960-66, General Electric has changed the method of performance appraisal. The twin objectives of the performance appraisal program—letting a man know where he stands via ratings and salary action, and motivating him to improve—were not being achieved by the methods used at General Electric. The results of the research "showed that attempts to achieve the first objective frequently produce threat and defensiveness and these reactions, in turn, interfere with the achievement of the second objective," notes the company report.[51] In the study it was found by accident that, contrary to corporate policy, managers generally did not hold performance appraisals unless pressured into having them. In the traditional company method of appraisal, the performance was evaluated and goals were set. Meyer notes, "Performance appraisal is authoritarian. There is no doubt who is boss and who is subordinate."[52] He also noted that the appraisal is highly emotional and managers find it hard to discuss negative performance. It was found that frequently a manager would admit to a third party that he considered a particular employee poor and desired to eliminate him, yet this would not be transmitted to the particular employee. The manager's appraisal interview often communicated just the opposite. Two years of research showed that employees were more sure of where they stood before having the appraisal interview than they were after the interview. In other words, the interview tended to confuse rather than clarify. Research also found that employees not having the interview (which was contrary to company policy but nonetheless common) desired to have an appraisal interview. Also, rarely was specific improvement discernible as a result of the interview.[53] Thus, the research concludes:

A merit-pay type of salary plan makes some variety of summary judgment or rating of performance necessary, or at least desirable; but this rating should *not* be expected to serve also as a primary medium for changing performance. Quite separate from this rating activity, the manager can use goal planning discussions, special assignments, and other techniques to achieve improved performance on the part of subordinates.[54]

Since 1966 the company has tried to use two or more interviews for performance appraisal. The first would be the discussion of past performance, and the results were used mainly for salary and rating needs. According to Meyer, this interview must be kept to a very short and not very comprehensive discussion. The other interviews are to deal with the future rather than the past. The function of the future-oriented interviews is to motivate the employee by mutually setting short-term measurable targets or objectives. Meyer, Kay, and French believe that three months usually is long enough for such targets. The study found, says Dr. Meyer, "only in those areas with specific targets were changes in performance observable and the more specific an objective the better."[55] They also believe that projects form better goals than day-to-day work. For instance, in a performance interview with a secretary it would be better to place a three-month goal to reorganize the files than to plan to have better daily typing.

The most constructive finding of the study was the fact that work-planning and goal-setting and subsequent review of progress discussions between managers and their subordinates, which focused on specific short-term plans and goals, yielded much greater returns in improved job performance than did appraisal discussions.[56] Since 1966, the company has tried to implement the goal-setting interview separate from the salary-appraisal review discussions. Periodic reviews of progress in achieving goals are used to provide a natural opportunity for mutual problem solving and a less threatening atmosphere than was characteristic of the salary review.

Because of the work by Meyer and his team, and by other behavioral scientists during the 1950s and sixties, General Electric made changes in the way work was assigned, accepted, and measured. The work-planning-and-review process consists of periodic, informal meetings between a man and his manager. There still are a few formal ratings, but the emphasis is on an attempt to get together informally to match evaluations and expectations in less quantitative terms. The process centers on helping a man observe and measure himself in terms of how well he is meeting his goals and deadlines. The review with the manager is then just confirmation of his own evaluation of his own performance.

Three basic assumptions underlie the review process in General Electric: an employee needs to know what is expected of him; an employee needs to know how he is doing; an employee needs to be able to obtain assistance when it is necessary.[57] The third assumption requires a climate that will encourage the individual to ask for assistance when necessary.

One General Electric study brought out that failures in any one of these assumptions were the causes for unfavorable attitudes held by highly valued engineers who later quit their jobs.[58]

Although the work of Meyer and his associates shows great promise, it has not convinced all authoritative behaviorists. Rensis Likert claimed, as recently as 1970, that General Electric departmental level practices his System I Management.[59] This generalization was made without qualification. He said that the stated philosophy of the firm is his System IV. In summary, from Likert's well-known book, *New Patterns of Management*, System I is a task-oriented, highly structured exploitive authoritarian management style, while System IV is a relationships-oriented or participative management style based on teamwork, mutual trust, and confidence.[60] Systems II and III, benevolent authoritarian and consultative, are intermediate stages. The two extremes, Systems I and IV, approximate closely the managerial styles described by McGregor's Theory X and Theory Y assumptions.[61]

Upon further probing, Likert was unable to present adequate research to substantiate his claim. He was able to note only two points in support of his statement. First, he said that General Electric in 1958 fired sixty managers for not making 6 percent return on investment. Second, he noted a study, undated, he had heard about covering three or four hundred General Electric engineers who were divided into four quartiles. The quartiles were arranged by subjective evaluation of their potential in the company's future. Likert said that half of all the engineers left the firm, and almost all of these engineers came from the quartile having the highest potential in the company's future. Again, no source, other than rumor, substantiates the evidence. Thus, Likert concluded that General Electric was not practicing System IV Management, but was practicing System I below the departmental level.

The department level is the profit center. As to its being autocratic in management practice, this could be the case at any point in time. If so, it would be contrary to the basic philosophy of the company, but it still would not be impossible to conceive. Leadership style is an individual attribute. Frequently, those who are autocratic don't even know they are, since at the same time they are teaching democratic leadership or leadership by persuasion. With about two hundred department general managers it is conceivable that a number of them could be autocratic, just as some are democratic. But to conclude that the department managers in General Electric were practicing System I Management based on only the two cited studies may be overgeneralizing.

The belief that the departments are headed by autocratic managers is not substantiated by other managers who have worked for General Electric. They admit that some managers were and are autocratic, but these are in the minority and frequently do not last long.[62] Greenwood denied that sixty managers were fired for not getting 6 percent return on investment.[63] He says, "I don't believe it. That many might have been fired, but certainly not for that reason." Greenwood says he has never heard of the study about three hundred engineers, but does not deny the point. "Of those employees in high level positions, the firm usually lost many whom it wanted to keep because they were the more aggressive ones," he says. Thus, it is admitted that those lost to the firm frequently are those most wanted. Greenwood, who has spent over a decade in personnel with the Chase Manhattan Bank, N.A., says that employees who quit on their own volition are usually persons of high quality, while employees of low or marginal quality are forced to resign or are fired. Greenwood goes on to assert that General Electric has a vast pool of capable people, and that the quality of professional people remains very high, since the weaker ones are continuously removed from employment and the strong ones compete against each other for the top positions.

Donald R. Webb agrees with the sentiments of a number of other people in claiming that General Electric before reorganization was a company practicing good human relations.

There used to be a widespread belief that General Electric was a Company with a conscience. There seemed to be a spirit pervading the Company—never expressly stated—which above all respected the dignity of human beings and which derived its basic policies, written or not written, from a higher order of principles. It is difficult to say where this spirit originated, but unquestionably it was a reflection of the high moral standards of its leaders. Undoubtedly, it was cemented together and communicated throughout the Company by the pep talks of the Company leaders at Association Island camps.[64]

As some people have classified the business climates in various companies and in various industries, General Electric was characterized by a general climate of "human warmth"—by a "soft" management. The climate varied in different parts of the company. For example, if the old Apparatus Departments were characterized by a "soft" management, Electronics was, by contrast, "hard." These variations were a reflection of the differences in competition and maturity of the industries in which the various parts of the company competed, as well as a reflection of the personalities of the leaders in the different parts of the company.[65]

The new organization and management philosophy that accompanied decentralization gave "scientific" legitimacy to much of this character. "Man-to-man discussions" were begun and were a part of the philosophy of the new salary plan. This is one excellent example of the action required by the new philosophy working in the direction of full recognition of the dignity of the human being and the desire to practice good human relations as understood in 1951 and the years following. Even some of the practices which appear on the surface to be "cold" are upon careful analysis practices which would further the "human warmth" of the managerial climate. For example, the philosophy made obsolete the practice of "kicking a man upstairs," which was actually much more harmful to him and to those around him than the frankness required by the new philosophy.

7

Entrepreneurship Planning and Decentralization

General Electric and all business organizations live within a changing economy and a changing technology. In a group of essays entitled *Technology, Management and Society*, Drucker argues convincingly that "up to the seventeenth century it was the purpose of all human institutions to prevent change."[1] Change was a threat to human security. But, he says, "In the business enterprise we have the first institution which is designed to produce change."[2] It is not the purpose here to agree or disagree with Drucker; it is only important to note the dynamics of the environment in which business lives. In a dynamic environment a business, in order to survive, must itself be dynamic. It must innovate; it must change to meet the changing requirements of survival. Drucker believes, "An organization structure must be temporary."[3] He says that our environment is in such a state of flux that "one is committed to changing an organization continuously. It is that dynamic."[4]

After the organization structure was well developed on paper around 1953, Ralph Cordiner asked Paul Mills if he thought General Electric organization structure needed any major revisions. Mills answered:

I think we ought to continue the study of the impact of "happening" [happening meaning the dynamics of the environment]. That so far as major revisions, I can't foresee any for another doubling in size of this company. And when this company doubles, I'm not so sure that this is the organization we should have.[5]

General Electric has more than doubled since Mills's statement, yet there has been almost no major change in the structure or philosophy. Growth has added a number of departments, from approximately eighty to about two hundred, and the groups have increased from five to eleven and back down to ten.

A student of organization might focus on the fact that today, save for size, GE's organization structure looks substantially like that of Cordiner's day. Recently, however, the firm restructured the Executive Office. In 1951 Cordiner set up an advisory organization made up of all group vice presidents and Services vice presidents. That structure was not altered until 1967, when Borch believed he could not handle this organization alone and he structured a smaller organization to oversee the Executive Office, made up of four other men, and called it the President's Office. (Later, with the death of Phillippe in 1968, the title changed to the Corporate Executive Office. This has been detailed in

Chapter 3.) In 1970 Borch added more advisory committees, all subdivisions of the Executive Office. He has the Corporate Administrative Staff, which coordinates functions ranging from accounting and legal operations to employee relations. He also has the Corporate Executive Staff, charged with investigating the effective use of resources and long-range plans with operating groups. These committees represent a break from company philosophy, which rejects the use of decision-making committees. Officially these committees are only advisory, but it is felt that realistically they are policy-making.[6]

General Electric has long been aware that it cannot afford the luxury of romantics who live by the philosophy "I don't know where I am going, but I'll get there one day soon."[7] Until recently, however, entrepreneurial planning seemed lacking, and in the opinion of many experts it seemed that the emphasis was on short-range profitability.[8] The natural tendency to try to avoid as much risk as possible has caused the company's management to look to new methods of forcing the implementation of venture management. The company understands that it cannot be more concerned with avoiding mistakes than with taking the right risks. Since "structure follows strategy and not the other way around," as Drucker notes,[9] the company must find the philosophy and organization to force emphasis on the long range. Alfred Chandler's research showed that structure is forced on the company by strategy made to fit the outside.[10] Yet it should be emphasized that organization is not a panacea; it is not a solution to General Electric's venture management problem. "The purpose of organization," as Drucker told me, "is not to solve problems, but to put the attention of the people in the organization in the right places, instead of the wrong places."[11] Chandler found "that the company's strategy in time determined its structure and that the common denominator of structure and strategy has been the application of the enterprise's resources to market demand."[12] He was also able to conclude, "structure has been the design for integrating the enterprise's existing resources to current demand; strategy has been the plan for the allocation of resources to anticipated demand."[13]

Where is General Electric heading? Peter Drucker believes we are entering an era where the emphasis in industry will be on entrepreneurship. He says, "It will not be the entrepreneurship of a century ago, that is, the ability of a single man to organize a business he himself could run, control, embrace. It will be rather the ability to create and direct an organization for the new."[14] The belief is that the new entrepreneurship will be built on top of the present managerial foundation.

Recent articles on General Electric have concentrated on failures of the company in the area of entrepreneurship or venture management.[15] John B. McKitterick, General Electric Vice President—Corporate Planning, believes these failures have pointed up the major problem the company faces, and this problem has been caused in part by inadequate development of the requirements needed to encourage venture management in the philosophy of the firm. Equally to blame for the lack of new ventures, claims McKitterick, is the fact that few people truly recognize what real "venture management" means.[16] He realizes that the philosophy that stressed the importance of balancing short- and long-range goals was not emphasizing anything like "venture management." What happened in the philosophy, and what management today sees as long-range planning, is really just extending the present into the future. That is to say, the company takes its present products and departments and tries to estimate how they will grow. But venture management is the job of directing resources from today into tomorrow. More important, unlike the traditional concept of long-range planning, venture management emphasis is not on minimizing risks, but rather maximizing opportunities.

Management literature has concentrated on what might be called the "administrative" part of the job. The emphasis since Taylor and Fayol has been on how humans and materials could be organized and how managers could lead more effectively. Little attention has been paid to the entrepreneurial side of the managerial function. Unfortunately, "the old folklore which says that existing businesses are incapable of doing the really new things has so far been proved," says Drucker.[17] The important point is that if the entrepreneurial function is to play such an important role in the future as Drucker, among others, believes must be the case, then management must know how to handle this function. The management of the entrepreneurial function requires a different kind of organization structure than was found in the company's decentralization plan as developed in the 1950s. Drucker concurs: "The managerial and the entrepreneurial [functions] are not organized in the same way. They require that, in our minds, we keep them not separate but, at least, distinct."[18] Managerial organizations are responsible for exploiting what is already in existence. That is not to say that they can't extend or improve. Yet organizations must learn to be entrepreneurial.

General Electric has a research staff in each area, but the firm is only beginning to see the need for a methodology for true venture management. To have a truly venture management organization, top management must think totally in terms of innovation and the future. It cannot be tied to any function or group. Venture management is first a state of mind, and managers who are tied to functional areas or groups have to successfully develop the venture management viewpoint. Development of different measuring devices for this side of the organization are also required. The present eight key result areas do not work as measurements for innovation—they perpetuate the existing structure of products. The key result areas of measurement are aimed at the managerial organizations, as opposed to the entrepreneurial side. Drucker was speaking to this point as early as 1950:

So far we have practically no measurements and controls in the enterprise. . . . We do not even have a reasonable gauge of productivity; for accounting . . . is by definition focused in the past rather than on the future.[19]

Later, he said, "In the enterprise the management job consists very largely of the management of change, if not of taking the lead in changes. Neither seniority nor the yardstick of a traditional pattern can be applied."[20] One President of General Electric claimed that the executive of the future will be judged largely by his skill in managing change.[21] Yet this is at present unmeasurable, and because other measurements are used to evaluate top executives, they concentrate on other duties. Managers tend to emphasize the part of their job on which they are measured. If General Electric wants to have a select group concentrate on venture management, they cannot be measured by the company's traditional eight key result areas.

On May 22, 1970, General Electric organized the Corporate Executive Staff, which was to advise the Executive Office on effective use of resources and review long-range plans. Its basic responsibility is to promote venture management.[22] The actual functioning of this body is still unclear, since the membership is comprised of vice presidents and managers of the staff components, and these men will retain their responsibility in each of their respective components. It would appear that the members of this committee have only a secondary responsibility to entrepreneurship and a primary responsibility to a particular component. As yet, no method of evaluating the work of the Corporate Executive Staff has been developed. This staff will think for the future, but top management is not sure what to expect from them. Very little is known about the workings of this Corporate Executive Staff as no literature, save for a few press releases, is available. McKitterick helped to show the need and then organize this venture management planning staff. He says he is glad the corporation understands the vital need for such an organization; now the requirement is to learn how such a structure should function. McKitterick sees the new staff committee as the best method for keeping GE as dynamic as its environment.[23]

To determine whether or not the new Corporate Executive Staff is a revolutionary change in the corporate structure will take a few years. The staff may end up functioning as another long-range planning organization based on traditional long-range planning methods, or it may truly be a corporate innovation, planning and fostering venture management. Only time will tell.

8   Conclusion

As this book defines it, decentralization to some extent characterizes all organizations. With such a broad interpretation of decentralization, most major firms could be termed decentralized, as Chandler, Dale, and Koontz and O'Donnell have pointed out. This interpretation was narrowed when managerial decentralization was introduced as being the development of a number of independent profit-and-loss centers within a larger organization, and further defined as being the process of how authority is delegated rather than how activities are grouped.

Decentralization as a philosophy dates back many years. It became well publicized with the reorganizing of the highly centralized DuPont Company into a decentralized unit, and later by the recentralizing of the extremely decentralized General Motors Corporation in the 1920s. The definition of decentralization differs from firm to firm. In Chapters 2 through 7 I presented decentralization as it is practiced in only one company—General Electric.

The General Electric decentralization has been discussed in the literature for a number of years; perhaps only the General Motors organization is discussed more frequently. General Electric decentralized in 1951, at the beginning of the decentralization fad which spread throughout industry after World War II and lasted to the beginning of the 1960s. This was three decades after the General Motors' experiment, so General Electric had the advantage of studying General Motors, which it did, in depth. General Electric also made a formal investigation of the organization needs of the corporation to develop a plan by which the company could institute decentralization. This formal study, headed by Ralph J. Cordiner, then Assistant to the President, lasted from 1943 through 1950, and was his *only* job. In 1951, he became President of General Electric Company and put the results of this eight-year study into effect.

The third chapter presented the managerial theory and the overall organizational structure. Here the concept of operations, services, and executive office was explained, as was the point that services do not make decisions for the line, but should only advise. It was also shown that GE does not use decision-making committees, and does not consider the Executive Office as a decision-making committee. Here, too, the organization structure was explained.

Chapter 4 detailed how the company proposes to measure the effectiveness of each area. Almost all of this measurement work is concentrated on the operating departments, and very little has been thought through for anyone other than an operating department general manager.

In the fifth chapter, I tried to show factual problems as encountered when the theory, knowledge, and concepts of the philosophy were exposed to the day-to-day operation of the organization. During the first decade of decentralization (1950-60) a conflict occurred between the "old guard" and the "new breed." The "old guard" had developed its managerial habits before decentralization, while the "new breed" became disciples of the new philosophy. A "cultural" clash developed and was only resolved as the "old guard" retired and the "new breed" rose in the ranks of the company. The actual organization structure was implemented by the mid-1950s, but it was only about 1960 that the decentralization philosophy was truly practiced on a wide basis. The belief by many managers that profitability was the only really important measurement also developed in the early 1950s. This belief that profitability is a more important measurement area than the other seven key result areas lingers to this day, even though the official voice of the company has emphatically claimed for almost twenty years that all eight key result areas have equal importance. In recent years this belief has been given some impetus by top management's desire to get current profits to cover unplanned financial needs.

Chapter 7 explored a recent organizational change, which hopes to insure that entrepreneurship will be encouraged on the executive level. In 1970 Borch set up a committee with the responsibility to administer the needs GE has in the area of venture management. After three years it is still too early to determine whether or not it represents any fundamental change in the philosophy or structure of the firm.

The plan, philosophy, and subsequent organization developed by General Electric for decentralization was the focal point of this book. The thinking that led the company to decide to decentralize is not of major importance, for it had little other choice, if we are to believe the writings of Cordiner, Smiddy, and Wilson. The bureaucracy of centralization had become an overbearing burden for one man to handle, a point that Wilson and Cordiner understood in the 1940s. The significant contribution to management theory was not the decision to decentralize, but what they did after the decision. The massive plan and philosophy, the thinking through of the general scope of management, and the organization theory itself comprise the contribution that the company has made to the general knowledge of formal organization.

This study has attempted to communicate a number of points. First, decentralization at GE was shown to be the building up of about two hundred individual profit centers, each having almost complete authority over production and merchandising of its products. Decentralization at General Electric was shown to revolve around these profit centers.

Emphasis was placed on the Cordiner years because it was in those years that the foundation was laid, the organization formed, the theory developed. Speaking of these years and the reorganization, Philip Reed said:

In 1950, when Ralph Cordiner first did it [decentralized], there was great resistance. But General Electric would never have grown as it has—lacking decentralization. It is just physically impossible, in my judgment, for any man or small group of men ... smart enough to know intimately all the things you should to make intelligent decisions in the marketplace, in your procurement, in your labor relations, in all the varied industries in which we participate.

The second thing is the decision-making opportunity such a system provides for people. It provides us with a mechanism by which authority can be given and measured. The individual will know whether he has succeeded or has failed.[1]

A second point developed was that the decentralization philosophy was adopted only after deep debate, long consideration, and extremely full visible experience with a highly centralized business bureaucracy with which General Electric had to struggle through the 1940s. General Electric's organization structure and philosophy was thought through, unlike the Westinghouse style, which according to Chandler was conceived in the 1930s and developed through a certain amount of trial and error.[2]

The important point about theory, as the company understands it, is that it is not separate from, but really a basic part of, good business practice. In the "Introduction to the Policy Volume" of the *General Electric Organization & Policy Guide*, the following statement is made:

As will be made clear, what are usually termed policies are in reality definitions of common purposes, which have been mutually agreed upon and accepted for the protection and preservation of the common interests of individuals, components, departments, the company and society in general.

The realization of common interests in free society, under the accepted principle of government by the consent of the governed, has involved the voluntary surrender of certain freedoms by individuals, in return for which they have received guarantees under laws protecting their individual rights. The right to make changes in these laws is assured under constitutional processes. The realization of common interests within the General Electric Company involves similar voluntary surrender by individuals engaged in working in, or responsible for managing, decentralized components. A similar right and responsibility to suggest changes, or make recommendations regarding the nature or impact of common interests, exists within the Company.[3]

The common purposes of the General Electric Company are very clearly defined in the written statement of company objectives and in General Electric's *Professional Management* series, in Cordiner's and Smiddy's speeches, which have been reprinted and widely distributed in the literature distributed within the company, and in many other similar documents. Most of the philosophy was developed and distributed before Borch became President and the changes which current Chairman of the Board Jones has made do not alter the philosophy. If one sifts through this literature and reads carefully, one finds a clear and consistent philosophy behind General Electric that meets all the requirements for defining "common purposes . . . for the protection and preservation of the common interests of individual . . . and society in general."

The thorough and deep thinking that has gone into the preparation of the philosophy described in Chapters 3, 4, and 5 is one of the most significant efforts that has ever been made in defining the common purposes of a large organization.

The organization structure and the philosophy which controls its work are well planned and well written, yet subject to change. Because of the dynamics of the firm, the philosophy must be somewhat fluid, and strongly structured at the same time. The amount of written documents the company has produced to control the system may seem excessive. But it is in these written forms that the company broadens the base of learning in its quest to lead its managers out of confusion. The written policies, procedures, and management books and letters represent simplification. Confusion existed in the absence of a written philosophy before 1950 under centralization. The development, teaching, and implementation of the philosophy brought some understanding of the practice and scope of professional management in General Electric. General Electric's internationally famous metallurgist and former Vice President, Zay Jeffries, in a personal letter to Harold Smiddy, explained the need for this simplification.

It is obvious that life is becoming more complex as our industrial civilization advances. The sum total of knowledge is increasing at a very rapid rate. . . . At the same time human beings are changing very little. There is no positive evidence that the more able men today excel the more able men of yesteryear.

The whole situation would, therefore, get out of hand and become unmanageable if it were not for the fact that, concurrently with the increase in complexity, there is also constant progress toward simplification.

Our progress depends to a considerable extent on seeing to it that the simplification processes move forward in approximate balance with the complicating processes, (so that) individuals do not become casualties of their own complexities.[4]

Smiddy frequently quoted this personal letter which, in a practical sense, may have inspired his intense pursuit of developing a sound fundamental approach toward managing and organizing the decentralized General Electric Company.

The investment in talent and time devoted to this research was very great. As to whether it was worth the effort no one can fairly judge, since no comparative analysis covering the same time span is possible. In spite of the tremendous strides made in the overall practice of management, there still is no clear-cut evidence that at General Electric Company the control function is any different or better today than it was prior to the decentralization of the managerial function. Mills may be right when he says, "I don't think a damn thing changed, they [top management] never lost centralized financial control; it was there before, and is there today. Although there are sharper tools today and data gathering is easier, its vast size merely balances the scale. Control is still at the top."[5]

A third point was that decentralization took years to implement and had many difficulties to overcome. Here it should be noted that the philosophy in written form was developed over a number of years; in fact, it is still developing. The measurement study, which began its investigation almost twenty years ago, is yet to be completed. The actual organization structure, which began in 1951, was only basically completed in 1955, although a number of changes took place after that, as discussed. It was Smiddy who admitted, although the philosophy was well publicized by 1955, that decentralization was only just beginning to be practiced at his retirement in 1961. The difficulty in putting into practice real decentralization was caused, as presented in Chapter 5, by the cultural clash, the one-measurement concept, misforecasting, and failure to have the philosophy completely developed.

Also important to understand is the fact that it cannot be determined whether or not decentralization caused the firm to grow faster or slower. The feelings of Cordiner, Smiddy, and Phillippe, and so forth, as previously quoted, indicate that decentralization has helped the firm financially. The 1950s, under decentralization, was a period of the greatest growth in the company's history.

This investigation was framed basically as a case study; therefore, there are not many independent conclusions to be drawn. Although most of the conclusions are left to the readers, some comments might be helpful.

Without doubt, General Electric is a bigger and more complex organization now than it was before decentralization. Drucker has called GE the most conglomerate of all conglomerates, and Northrup and Cordiner described it as the most diversified firm in the world. In spite of many profit centers, the organization structure does not seem too complicated. Chapter 3 contains a description of the three branches—services, operations, and the executive office. It is important to note that in this huge corporation comprising many businesses, for the most part, only five to seven levels of management exist, and that there are only ten groups and fewer than two hundred departments.

The depth and scope of the theory behind the structure is, in my opinion, outstanding and extremely sound. The quality of the theory is not evaluated against those practiced by other firms, such as IBM or General Motors, which would be a subject for another book. The discussion of the philosophy as found in this volume is intended to show the wide scope and depth of that formalized managerial approach. It is concluded, by this writer, that the General Electric philosophy of management is built upon a solid foundation of research. The fact that it has changed very little since it was introduced may be significant substantiation of its conceptual soundness.

On the other hand, it is important to note that all of the managerial theory covered in the philosophy is not practiced. The concept of eight key result areas for measuring an operating department and its manager has, in reality, never been practiced. Profitability still seems to be the dominating key result area. Vice Chairman of the Board Jack S. Parker admitted that profitability during the 1960s dominated the other measurements. There is no evidence that it is not today's primary concern. With all the emphasis on measuring managers on their performance, it is interesting that the only measurements that have been developed to any extent are applicable to operations solely. The measurements of services and the functional areas along with individual contributions above or below the profit center level have not been developed as yet. Therefore, after twenty years of researching and practicing its decentralization philosophy, General Electric has not developed a sound, generally acceptable measurement for any manager, consultant, or high-level individual contributor, other than the manager of a profit center. There are less than two hundred of these positions out of over 400,000 employees.

It is generally agreed that the General Electric Company was highly successful before decentralization in the 1920s, 1930s, and 1940s, and that since decentralization during the 1950s and 1960s it has outstripped its nearest competitors. It has more than doubled in sales in each decade since decentralization. If the stock market can be used as a barometer of public confidence in General Electric's management, including its philosophy and structure, then its future looks bright. Whether its control function is better or worse, or has changed significantly or not since decentralization is not clear, except that profitability measurements have been more carefully spelled out for managers of all operation components.

Mary Parker Follett once said, "Business practice has gone ahead of Business Theory."[6] Whether or not she was correct when she made that observation in 1926, or if the statement is correct today, is outside the boundaries of this book. It is important to understand what practitioners have done and what theory they have developed. Through the understanding of what others think and do, it may be possible to advance the general theory of management beyond the present. This book was written with that hope in mind. Some of the most influential thinkers in the early history of management thought were themselves managers— Taylor, Fayol, Barnard, Towne, Roundtree, to name but a few—but in recent years it seems that most of the influential writers are academicians and consultants—Dale, Drucker, Koontz, Argyris, Likert, and so forth—and perhaps the modern theoretician does not appreciate the quality of the theory being developed by managers themselves. The General Electric philosophy of management was developed by managers, managers who read the classics in management and who consulted with many of the most important academic writers; yet the managers who developed the GE structure and managerial theory were men who for most of their lives had been operating managers. Over years of on-the-job experience, trial and error, and formal training, these men had acquired a very substantial reputation as successful leaders, managers, and thinkers. Therefore, the deep thought that went into the General Electric organization and philosophy was founded in operating knowledge which may have helped to add insight, but also may have added prejudice to what was the final product.

Notes

Notes

Preface

1. See Chapter 1 of the book.

2. Interview with Peter F. Drucker, New York, November 2, 1970.

3. Theodore K. Quinn, *Unconscious Public Enemies* (New York: The Citadel Press, 1962), pp. 112-13.

4. Interview with Peter F. Drucker, New York, November 2, 1970.

5. *General Electric Company Annual Reports*, 1950, 1960, 1970.

6. Alfred Chandler, Jr., *Strategy and Structure: Chapters in the History of the Industrial Enterprise* (Cambridge, Mass.: The M.I.T. Press, 1962), p. 365.

7. Letter from Charles E. Wilson, April 14, 1970.

8. *Professional Management in General Electric Book One: General Electric's Growth* (New York: General Electric Company, 1953), p. 3.

9. Chandler, p. 369.

Chapter 1
Decentralization

1. Alfred D. Chandler, Jr., "Management Decentralization: A Historical Analysis," *The History of American Management Selections from the Business History Review*, ed. by James P. Baughman (Englewood Cliffs, N.J.: Prentice-Hall, Inc., 1969). (First appeared vol. 30, June 1956.)

2. Ibid., p. 241.

3. Decentralization in American industry can be traced before 1900 in the transportation, utility, and financial industries.

4. Donaldson Brown's best-known work is "Decentralized Operations and Responsibilities with Coordinated Control," *Annual Convention Series*, no. 57 (New York: American Management Association, 1927).

5. See especially Ralph Cordiner, *New Frontiers for Professional Managers* (New York: McGraw-Hill Book Company, Inc., 1956) and his two articles in the *General Management Series*, American Management Association, no. 134, "The Implications of Industrial Decentralization" (1945); and no. 159, "Problems of Management in a Large Decentralized Organization" (1952).

6. Ernest Dale's three leading works on organizational structure are: *Planning and Developing the Company Organization Structure*, Research Report no. 20 (New York: American Management Association, 1952) (this book is outstanding for its research); *Organizations* (New York: American Management Association, 1967), Chapter 6; *The Great Organizers* (New York: McGraw-Hill Book Company, Inc., 1960). See also his short but comprehensive article

published in numerous books of management readings, "Centralization Versus Decentralization," *Advanced Management*, vol. 20 (June 1955), pp. 11-16 (published under a different title in Europe in 1954).

7. See John Dearden, "Problem In Decentralized Profit Responsibility," *Harvard Business Review*, vol. 38, no. 3 (May-June 1960), pp. 79-86; "Problem in Decentralized Financial Control," *Harvard Business Review*, vol. 39, no. 3 (May-June 1961), pp. 72-80; "Mirage of Profit Decentralization," *Harvard Business Review*, vol. 40, no. 6 (November-December 1962), pp. 140-54; "Limits on Decentralized Profit Responsibility," *Harvard Business Review*, vol. 40, no. 4 (July-August 1962), pp. 81-89.

8. See Alfred P. Sloan, Jr., *My Years with General Motors* (New York: Doubleday and Company, 1964).

9. See Dale, *Planning and Developing the Company Organization Structure*, Stage VI; H.J. Kruisinga, *The Balance Between Centralization and Decentralization in Managerial Control* (Leiden: H.E. Stenfest Kroese N.V., 1954), p. 3; Dearden, "Mirage of Profit Decentralization," p. 141; *Decentralization in Industry: Studies in Business Policy*, no. 30 (New York: National Industrial Conference Board, 1948), p. 3.

10. Dale, "Centralization Versus Decentralization," p. 11.

11. Harold Koontz and Cyril O'Donnell, *Principles of Management: An Analysis of Managerial Functions*, fourth ed. (New York: McGraw-Hill Book Company, Inc., 1968), p. 349.

12. Henri Fayol, *General and Industrial Management*, trans. by Constance Storrs (London: Sir Isaac Pitman and Sons, Ltd., 1949), p. 33.

13. Ibid.

14. Ibid., p. 34.

15. Dale, *Planning and Developing the Company Organization Structure*, p. 118.

16. Ibid.

17. Henry H. Albers, *Principles of Organization and Management*, second ed. (New York: John Wiley & Sons, 1965).

18. Helen Baker and Robert R. France, *Centralization and Decentralization in Industrial Relations* (Princeton, N.J.: Industrial Relations Section, Department of Economics and Sociology, Princeton University, 1954).

19. Meyer N. Zald, "Decentralization—Myth vs. Reality," *Personnel*, vol. 41, no. 4 (July-August 1964).

20. Peter F. Drucker, *The Practice of Management* (New York: Harper & Brothers, 1954), pp. 205-7.

21. Ibid., p. 208.

22. Ibid., p. 205.

23. Ibid.

24. Brown, p. 14.

25. See Chandler; Dale, *The Great Organizers;* Drucker, *The Practice of*

Management; and *Concept of the Corporation* (New York: John Day Company, 1946; second ed. 1972).

26. Chandler, pp. 188-89, is quoted as found, changing only from past tense to present tense.

27. Bernard H. Baum, *Decentralization of Authority in a Bureaucracy* (Englewood Cliffs, N.J.: Prentice-Hall, Inc., 1961), p. 22.

28. Harold Stieglitz, *Organization Planning Basic Concepts Emerging Trend* (New York: National Industrial Conference Board, 1968), p. 5.

29. James D. Mooney and Alan C. Riley, *The Principles of Organization* (New York: Harper & Brothers, 1939), p. 17.

30. Ralph Currier Davis, *The Fundamentals of Top Management* (New York: Harper & Row, 1951), p. 307.

31. Stieglitz, p. 20.

32. Dale, *Planning and Developing the Company Organization Structure*, p. 107.

33. Dale, *Planning and Developing the Company Organization Structure*, p. 110.

34. Ibid., p. 111.

35. Henry L. Sisk, *Principles of Management: A Systems Approach to the Management Process* (Cincinnati: Southwestern Publishing, 1969), pp. 328-29.

36. Koontz and O'Donnell, pp. 352-53.

37. Ibid., p. 353.

38. George A. Smith, Jr., "Centralization and Decentralization," *A Management Sourcebook*, ed. by Franklin G. Moore (New York: Harper & Row, 1964), p. 257. Also noted by Keith Davis, *Human Relations in Business* (New York: McGraw-Hill Book Co., 1957), p. 348.

39. Lounsbury S. Fish, "Decentralization Reappraised," *A Management Sourcebook*, ed. by Franklin G. Moore (New York: Harper & Row, 1964), p. 252.

40. Dale, *Planning and Developing the Company Organization Structure*, p. 38.

41. No attempt will be made to evaluate this in terms of the Peter Principle: "In a hierarchy every employee tends to rise to his level of incompetence," Laurence J. Peter and Raymond Hull, *The Peter Principle* (New York: William Morrow and Company, 1969), p. 25.

42. Koontz and O'Donnell, p. 353.

43. Ibid., p. 357.

44. Dale, "Centralization vs. Decentralization," p. 13.

45. Zald, p. 22.

46. Drucker, *The Practice of Management*, p. 214.

47. Drucker, *The Practice of Management*, p. 216.

48. Haimann, p. 246; see also Gerry E. Morse, "The Swinging Pendulum of Management Control," *Emerging Concepts In Management*, ed. by Max S. Wortman (New York: Macmillan Company, 1969).

49. Dale, *Planning and Developing the Company Organization Structure*, p. 122.

50. Ibid.

51. Harold J. Leavitt and Thomas L. Whisler, "Management in the 1980's," *Harvard Business Review*, vol. 36, no. 6 (November-December 1958), p. 43.

52. Gilbert Burck, "Management Will Never Be the Same Again," *Fortune*, vol. 70, no. 2 (August 1964), pp. 124-26ff.

53. Max Ways, "Tomorrow's Management: A More Adventurous Life in a Free-Form Corporation," *Fortune*, vol. 74, no. 1 (July 1, 1966), pp. 84-87.

54. H. Igor Ansoff, "The Firm of the Future," *Harvard Business Review*, vol. 43, no. 5 (September-October 1965). Also see John P. Burlingame, "Information Technology and Decentralization," *Decision Theory and Information Systems*, ed. by William T. Greenwood (Cincinnati: Southwestern Publishing, 1969), pp. 630-40.

55. John Dearden, "Computers: No Impact on Divisional Control," *Harvard Business Review*, vol. 45, no. 1 (January-February 1967), pp. 99-104.

56. Dale, *Organizations*, p. 122.

57. Ronald Greenwood, "Managerial Functions: A Classification of Major Contributions," *Arkansas Business and Economic Review*, vol. 2, no. 2 (May 1969), pp. 14-17.

58. Arnold F. Emich, "Control Means Action," *Harvard Business Review*, vol. 32, no. 4 (July-August 1954), pp. 92-98.

59. Peter F. Drucker, "Controls, Control and Management," *Management Controls*, ed. by Charles P. Bonin, Robert K. Jaedicke, and Harvey M. Wagner (New York: McGraw-Hill Book Company, Inc., 1964), p. 295.

60. Albers, p. 174.

61. Rensis Likert, *New Patterns of Management* (New York: McGraw-Hill Book Company, Inc., 1961), p. 85.

62. Brown, pp. 14-15.

Chapter 2
A Short History of the
General Electric Company

1. Jules Backman, *The Economics of the Electrical Machinery Industry* (New York: New York University Press, 1962), p. 23.

2. *General Electric Company Annual Report, 1972*, p. 38.

3. *Westinghouse Electric Corporation Annual Report, 1972.*

4. See *Fortune*, vol. 87, no. 5 (May 1973), p. 222.

5. *Professional Management in General Electric, Book One: General Electric's Growth* (New York: General Electric Company, 1953), p. 4.

6. David Loth, *Swope of G.E.* (New York: Simon and Schuster, 1958), pp. 4, 103.

7. International General Electric is a wholly owned subsidiary whose main function is to market GE products outside the United States.

8. Loth, p. 103.

9. Ibid., p. 109.

10. "GE's Third Generation: Wilson and Reed," *Fortune*, vol. 21, no. 1 (January 1940), p. 102.

11. Ibid., p. 68.

12. "Mr. Wilson at Work," *Fortune*, vol. 36, no. 5 (May 1947), p. 123.

13. Ibid., p. 166.

14. Ibid.

15. Ralph J. Cordiner, *New Frontiers for Professional Managers* (New York: McGraw-Hill Book Company, Inc., 1956), p. 11.

16. "Mr. Wilson at Work," p. 168.

17. Ibid.

18. Ibid., p. 168.

19. Herbert R. Northrup, *Boulwarism* (Ann Arbor, Mich.: University of Michigan, 1964), p. 3.

20. Cordiner, *New Frontiers for Professional Managers*, p. 16.

21. *General Electric Company Annual Report 1948*, p. 15.

22. Interview with Harold F. Smiddy, retired Vice President, Management Consultation Services, General Electric Company, Cincinnati, Ohio, August 24, 1969.

23. Frederick W. Cleveland, Jr., and Clarence C. Walton, *The Corporations on Trial: The Electric Cases* (Belmont, Calif.: Wadsworth Publishing Company, 1964), p. 63.

24. Edward M. Currie, "The Importance of Human Relations in Decentralization: A Study of G.E.," unpublished Master's thesis, Iowa State University, April 15, 1965, p. 1.

25. Ibid.

26. Ralph J. Cordiner, "The Implications of Industrial Decentralization," *General Management Series*, no. 134 (New York: American Management Association, 1945), p. 26.

27. *Professional Management in General Electric, Book One*, p. 42.

28. Currie, pp. 2-3. The $8000 average salary figure is the level reached in 1963. See *General Electric Company Annual Report 1963*, p. 32. More precisely, the average salary in 1948 was $3367, as figured from *General Electric Company Annual Report 1948*, p. 2.

29. See "G.E. Institute Nears End of Run—Now What?" *Business Week* (March 4, 1961), pp. 50-56, and "G.E.'s 'College' Is Back in Session," *Business Week* (February 8, 1964), pp. 78-79.

30. "Management Training: An Act of Faith," *Dun's Review*, vol. 92, no. 6 (December 1968), p. 47. The definition of three-deep is GE's own and should not be confused with more traditional definitions.

31. *Professional Management in General Electric Book Two: General Electric's Organization* (New York: General Electric Company, 1955), pp. 290-91.

32. Currie, p. 4.

33. Peter F. Drucker, *The Practice of Management* (New York: Harper & Brothers, 1954), pp. 282-84.

34. The works of Munsterberg, L. Gilbreth, and Lewin are not to be cast aside, but from the practitioners' side, human relations became a fad through the work of Mayo and Roethlisberger and the later researchers.

35. *Professional Management in General Electric Book One*, p. 45.

36. William B. Harris, "The Overhaul of General Electric," *Fortune*, vol. 52, no. 12 (December 1955), p. 115.

37. "Cordiner of General Electric," *Fortune*, vol. 45, no. 5 (May 1952), p. 157.

38. Currie, p. 6.

39. *General Electric Company Annual Report 1953*, p. 15.

40. Hurni is most likely the author of *The Next Step in Management. . . An Appraisal of Cybernetics*, General Electric Company, 1952.

41. *General Electric Company Annual Report 1952*, p. 2.

42. *General Electric Company Annual Report 1956*, p. 28.

43. Ralph J. Cordiner, "The Development of Companies," *Responsibilities of Business Leadership: Talks Presented at the Leadership Conferences, Association Island* (New York: General Electric Company, 1954), p. 13.

44. *General Electric Company Annual Report 1963*, p. 32.

45. *General Electric Company Annual Report 1969*, p. 36.

46. *General Electric Company Annual Report 1972*.

47. "General Electric: Two at the Top," *Forbes*, vol. 92, no. 8 (October 15, 1963), p. 17, and "G.E. Shifts Herald Harder Consumer-sell," *Business Week* (October 12, 1963), p. 88.

48. Interview with Harold F. Smiddy, Cincinnati, Ohio, August 24, 1969.

49. "As I See It: An Interview with Retired G.E. Chairman, Ralph Cordiner," *Forbes*, vol. 100, no. 8 (October 15, 1967), p. 37.

50. "G.E. Reshapes Divisions," *Business Week* (December 25, 1965), p. 20.

51. "G.E. Expands Its Top Echelon," *Business Week* (November 25, 1967), p. 46; see also, "G.E. Prepares Major Shifts," *Aviation Week and Space Technology*, vol. 87, no. 23 (December 4, 1967), p. 23.

52. *General Electric Company Annual Report 1967*, p. 25.

53. "A New Team Rewires G.E. for the Future," *Business Week* (March 30, 1968), p. 102.

54. "G.E. Expands Its Top Echelon," p. 46.

55. "A New Team Rewires G.E. for the Future," p. 106.

56. *General Electric Company Annual Report 1968*, p. 5.

57. "A New Team Rewires G.E. for the Future," p. 102.

58. Ibid.

59. Ibid., p. 109.

60. Fred Borch, "How Do You Keep Up with a Company That's Growing $1 Billion a Year?" *Forbes*, vol. 100, no. 6 (September 15, 1969), p. 336.

61. *General Electric Company Annual Reports 1950-1959.*

62. *General Electric Company Annual Reports 1960-1968.*

63. "G.E. Redesigns at the Top," *Business Week* (December 28, 1968), p. 24.

64. F.J. Borch, "Growth of the Company: 1900-2000," General Electric Company Speech to Elfun, July 15, 1968, p. 3.

65. *Thirty Year Review of the General Electric Company, 1892-1922* (Schenectady, N.Y.: General Electric Company, July 16, 1923), p. 4.

66. *General Electric Company Fifty-fifth Annual Report and Yearbook 1946*, p. 9.

67. Borch, p. 3.

68. "The Ten Best Managed Companies," *Dun's Review and Modern Industry*, vol. 81, no. 1 (January 1963), p. 86.

69. "General Electric's Old-Boy Club," *Dun's Review and Modern Industry*, vol. 92, no. 3 (October 1968), pp. 48-50.

70. Ibid., p. 49.

71. John Thackray, "Management Ways of General Electric," *Dun's Review and Modern Industry*, vol. 82, no. 5 (November 1963), p. 30.

Chapter 3
The Philosophy and Structure of the
General Electric Organization

1. *Professional Management in General Electric Book One: General Electric's Growth* (New York: General Electric Company, 1953), p. 25.

2. Ibid.

3. *Professional Management in General Electric Book Two: General Electric's Organization* (New York: General Electric Company, 1955), p. 99.

4. Ralph Cordiner, "Problems of Management in a Large Decentralized Organization," *General Management Series*, no. 159 (New York: American Management Association, 1952), pp. 13-14.

5. "GE Gets the Small-Business Touch," *Business Week*, April 19, 1952, p. 124.

6. Harold F. Smiddy and Paul E. Mills, "Discussion by Harold F. Smiddy and Paul E. Mills of Questions Raised by AMC—1956" (Crotonville, N.Y.: General Electric Company, 1956), pp. 16-17.

7. A.F. Vinson, "General Electric's Services Divisions," *Planning, Managing, and Measuring* (New York: Controllership Foundation, 1955), p. 9.

8. Ibid.

9. See Alfred P. Sloan, Jr., *My Years with General Motors* (New York: Doubleday and Company, 1964), especially Chapter 3, "Concept of the Organization." Also see Ernest Dale, *The Great Organizers* (New York: McGraw-Hill Book Company, Inc., 1960), Chapter 3, "Contributions to Organization and Administration by Alfred P. Sloan, Jr., and GM."

10. Peter F. Drucker, *Concept of the Corporation* (New York: John Day Company, 1946), p. 56.

11. John Thackray, "Management Ways of General Electric," *Dun's Review and Modern Industry*, vol. 82, no. 5 (November 1963), p. 68. Reprinted by special permission from *Dun's*, Dun & Bradstreet Publication Corp.

12. Ibid.

13. Peter F. Drucker, *Landmarks of Tomorrow* (New York: Harper & Brothers, 1959), p. 41.

14. *Professional Management in General Electric Book Two*, p. 120.

15. Ibid.

16. Ibid.

17. Interview with William J. Greenwood, Darien, Connecticut, October 19, 1968.

18. *Professional Management in General Electric Book Two*, p. 123.

19. "Services Officer Position Guide," *General Electric Organization and Policy Guide*, issued by Chairman of the Board and Chief Executive Officer, p. 1.

20. Lawrence M. Hughes, "G-E Under Decentralization Reaps Record Sales and Profits," *Sales Management*, vol. 80, no. 5 (March 7, 1958), p. 35. Reprinted by permission from *Sales Management*, The Marketing Magazine. Copyright 1958.

21. Ibid.

22. Ibid., p. 112.

23. Ibid.

24. Ibid.

25. Ibid.

26. Ibid.

27. Ibid., p. 114.

28. Ibid., p. 116.

29. Ibid.

30. Ralph J. Cordiner, *New Frontiers for Professional Managers* (New York: McGraw-Hill Book Company, Inc., 1956), p. 58.

31. See *Business Week*, February 3, 1951, p. 25; *Business Week*, June 9, 1951, p. 109; *Business Week*, December 10, 1955, p. 128; *Aviation Week and Space Technology*, vol. 87, no. 23 (December 4, 1967), p. 33; *Business Week*, December 25, 1965, p. 20; *Business Week*, April 19, 1969, p. 37.

32. *Professional Management in General Electric Book Two*, p. 135.

33. Harold F. Smiddy, "Profit Accountability, and Relationships Responsibilities, of Decentralized Product Operating Components; and Especially of 'Non-manufacturing' Business Components," *Addresses and Comments by Harold F. Smiddy on Organizing, Managing and Related Subjects*, vol. 2 (New York: General Electric Company, July 1958), p. 1.

34. For a detailed discussion of the organization structuring and philosophy,

General Electric prepared a manual of about 600 pages: *Manual of Organization Structuring Principles and Criteria Designed for Use in Operating Components of General Electric Company* (New York: Management Consultation Services, January 21, 1955; reprinted December 1957). The firm designed a like manual for Services Components (November 1957).

35. Harold F. Smiddy, "Automation," speech at Atlantic City Management Conference, General Electric Company, March 5, 1959. (Taken from recording of speech.)

36. Harry A. Hopf, *New Perspectives in Management* (Philadelphia: The Speculation, 1953), p. 194.

37. Cordiner, *New Frontiers for Professional Managers*, pp. 58-60.

38. "Lessons of Leadership: Part XXXIV: Inspiring Teamwork," *The Nation's Business*, vol. 56, no. 3 (March 1968), p. 44.

39. "Excerpts from Distributed Reports of General Electric Management Conferences," Appendix J, *Manual of Organization Structuring Principles and Criteria for Services Components of General Electric Company* (New York: General Electric Company, December 1958), pp. 5-6.

40. Ibid., p. 6.

41. *Individual Position and Organization Component Nomenclature* (New York: Management Consultation Services, General Electric Company, August 10, 1956), p. 105. For a fuller discussion of the individual contributor, see *Professional Management in General Electric, Book Four, The Work of a Functional Individual Contributor* (New York: General Electric Company, 1959).

42. Smiddy and Mills, p. 5.

43. Peter F. Drucker, *The Practice of Management* (New York: Harper & Row, 1954), p. 234.

44. Smiddy and Mills, pp. 4-6.

45. Ibid., p. 20. This statement is not to be confused with Barnard's and Argyris's belief of bottoms-up authority.

46. *Professional Management in General Electric Book Two*, p. 95.

47. Ibid., pp. 197-99.

48. Interview with William J. Greenwood, Honolulu, Hawaii, February 4, 1970.

49. Particularly Book Two.

50. Interview with William J. Greenwood, Honolulu, Hawaii, February 4, 1970.

51. Cordiner, *New Frontiers for Professional Managers*, pp. 70-71.

52. "Designing Work Into Positions and Grouping Positions Into Components," without publication data, internal General Electric working paper (pre-1960), p. 20.

53. Ibid.

54. Ray E. Brown, *Judgment In Administration* (New York: McGraw-Hill Book Company, Inc., 1966), p. 43.

55. Ibid., p. 77.

56. "Designing Work . . . ," p. 21.

57. Personal letter from Lieutenant Colonel Lyndall Urwick, June 24, 1969.

58. Ernest Dale and Lyndall F. Urwick, *Staff In Organization* (New York: McGraw-Hill Book Company, Inc., 1960), p. 159. This statement does not always apply and does not apply to subordinates to the "assistant to."

59. Urwick letter.

60. Ibid.

61. "Can Management Be Managed?" *Fortune*, vol. 48, no. 7 (July 1953), p. 141. The denial was made in a personal letter to this author dated October 27, 1973.

62. Harold F. Smiddy, "Some Notes on the Subject of 'Assistants' For, and To, Executives and Managers," July 5, 1952 (New York: Management Consultation Services Division, General Electric Company). (From notes made September 14, 1951.)

63. *Professional Management in General Electric Book Two*, p. 189.

64. Ibid., pp. 191-92.

65. Interview with William J. Greenwood, Honolulu, Hawaii, February 5, 1970.

66. Northcote Parkinson, *Parkinson's Law and Other Studies in Administration* (Boston: Houghton Mifflin Company, 1957), p. 4.

67. Urwick letter.

68. Cordiner, *New Frontiers for Professional Managers*, p. 70.

69. William T. Morris, *Decentralization in Management Systems: An Introduction to Design* (Columbus, Ohio: Ohio State University Press, 1968), p. 3.

70. Rocco Carzo, Jr., and John N. Yanouzas, *Formal Organization* (Homewood, Ill.: Richard D. Irwin, Inc., The Dorsey Press, 1967), p. 59.

71. Cordiner, *New Frontiers for Professional Managers*, p. 32.

72. Paul E. Mills, "Making Decentralization Work: One Company's Experience," *The Management Review*, vol. 46, no. 6 (June 1957), p. 70.

73. Quoted by Harold F. Smiddy, "Actually Doing 'The Work of a Professional Manager,'" (Crotonville, N.Y.: Advanced Management Course, February 21, 1956), p. 13.

74. Harold F. Smiddy, "Basis for the Development of General Electric's Management Philosophy," remarks to conference at Waldorf Astoria, New York, February 18, 1956, p. 4.

Chapter 4
Controlling Decentralization

1. Interview with Hugh Estes, New York, July 30, 1969.

2. Ralph J. Cordiner, "Problems of Management in a Large Decentralized

Organization," *General Management Series*, no. 159 (New York: American Management Association), p. 7.

3. *Measurements Project, Part I* (Schenectady, N.Y.: General Electric Company, January 1954), p. 5.

4. Robert W. Lewis, "Measuring, Reporting, and Appraising Results of Operation with Reference to Goals, Plans and Budgets," *Planning, Managing, and Measuring the Business: A Case Study of Management Planning and Control at General Electric Company* (New York: Comptrollership Foundation, 1955), pp. 29-30.

5. Ibid., p. 30.

6. Ibid., pp. 30-31.

7. Peter F. Drucker, *The Practice of Management* (New York: Harper & Brothers, 1954), p. 63.

8. Peter F. Drucker, *The New Society* (New York: Harper & Row, 1950), Chapter 4.

9. Peter F. Drucker, *The Practice of Management* pp. 70-77.

10. Ibid., p. 77.

11. *Measurements Project, Part II, Operational Measurements Key Result Area No. 1: Profitability* (Schenectady, N.Y.: General Electric Company, Budgets and Measurements Service Department, Accounting Services Division, January 1954), p. 3.

12. Ibid., p. 4.

13. Ibid.

14. Ibid., Sections 1 and 2.

15. Ibid., p. 7.

16. John Dearden, "Limits on Decentralized Profit Responsibility," *Harvard Business Review*, vol. 40, no. 4 (July-August 1962), p. 82.

17. *Measurements Project, Part II*, p. 37.

18. Ibid., pp. 24-25.

19. Interview with Maurice Mayo, New York, July 30, 1969.

20. The following is taken from the *Measurements Project* report on *Profitability* (January 1954).

21. Ibid., p. 27.

22. Walter Routenstrauch and Raymond Villers, *Budgetary Control* (New York: Funk and Wagnalls, 1957), p. 158. Also see Harold Bierman, Jr., and Allan R. Drebin, *Managerial Accounting: An Introduction* (New York: The Macmillan Company, 1968), pp. 224-47.

23. Peter F. Drucker, *Managing for Results: Economic Tasks and Risk-Taking Decisions* (New York: Harper & Row, 1964), pp. 29-30. The example may be drawn from General Electric.

24. *Measurements Project, Part II*, p. 30.

25. Ibid.

26. Ibid., p. 31.

27. Ibid., pp. 33-34.

28. Ibid., p. 36.

29. "Excerpts from the Measurements Project" (New York: Measurements Services Department, Accounting Services Division, General Electric Company, January 1954), fourth page (unnumbered).

30. Charles E. St. Thomas, "A Basic Guide to Marketing," *Modern Marketing Thought*, ed. by J.H. Westing and Gerald Albaum (New York: The Macmillan Company, 1964), p. 2.

31. Quoted by Harold F. Smiddy, "The Customer and the Business Process," speech delivered to Rotary Club, Louisville, Kentucky, January 13, 1955.

32. Drucker, *The Practice of Management*, p. 37; *Managing for Results* (New York: Harper and Row, 1957), p. 91.

33. Drucker, *The Practice of Management*, pp. 65-68.

34. "Excerpts from the Measurements Project."

35. Drucker, *The Practice of Management*, p. 67.

36. Drucker, *Managing for Results*, p. 95.

37. E. Jerome McCarthy, *Basic Marketing: A Managerial Approach*, rev. ed. (Homewood, Ill.: Richard D. Irwin, 1964), pp. 35-36.

38. Drucker, *Managing for Results*, pp. 93-94.

39. *Measurements Project Operational Measurements, Key Result Area No. 2: Market Position* (Schenectady, N.Y.: General Electric Company, April 1956), p. 5.

40. Ibid., pp. 5-6.

41. Ibid., p. 8.

42. Ibid., p. 19.

43. Ibid., pp. 20-21.

44. Ibid., p. 25. This concludes the illustration.

45. Peter F. Drucker, *The Age of Discontinuity* (New York: Harper & Row, 1969), p. 151.

46. Ibid.

47. "Productivity," *Relations News Letter* (New York: Relations Services, General Electric Company, August 1, 1960), p. 1.

48. *Measurements Project, Part I*, p. 12.

49. Ibid., p. 13.

50. Ibid.

51. Robert W. Lewis, "Measuring, Reporting and Appraising Results of Operations with Reference to Goals, Plans and Budgets," *Planning, Managing and Measuring the Business, A Case Study of Management Planning and Control at General Electric Company* (New York: Controllership Foundation, 1959), pp. 35-36.

52. Drucker, *Managing for Results*, p. 44.

53. Ibid., p. 43.

54. Ibid., p. 44.

55. *Measurements Project Operational Measurements Key Result Area No. 4: Product Leadership* (Schenectady, N.Y.: General Electric Company, April 1956), p. 2.

56. Ibid., p. 5.

57. "Excerpts from the Measurements Project," p. 5.

58. Theodore K. Quinn, *Giant Business: Threat to Democracy* (New York: Exposition Press, 1953), p. 117.

59. Drucker, *Managing for Results*, p. 115.

60. *Key Area: No. 4*, p. 19.

61. The most concise definition of General Electric's method of personnel development is found in Harold F. Smiddy, "General Electric's Philosophy and Approach for Manager Development," *General Management Series No. 174* (New York: American Management Association. 1955). Also see Gerald L. Phillippe, "Management Training at General Electric," *The Controller*, vol. 29, no. 8 (August 1961). General Electric has also published, for internal use only, the following books: *Manager Development Basic Principles and Plan* (1954), *Manager Development Guidebook I, Managerial Climate* (1954), *Manager Development Guidebook II, Self-Development Planning* (1954), *Manager Development Guidebook III, Manager Manpower Planning* (1954), *Manager Development Guidebook IV, Manager Education* (1954).

62. Edwin B. Flippo, *Principles of Personnel Management* (New York: McGraw-Hill Book Company, Inc., 1960), p. 218.

63. Ronald B. Shuman, Cross Professor of Management, University of Oklahoma, Norman, Oklahoma, lecture, April 24, 1967.

64. Peter F. Drucker, *The Effective Executive* (New York: Harper & Row, 1967), pp. 166-74.

65. *Key Result Area: No. 4*, p. 21.

66. Ibid.

67. Quoted in Herbert Harris, "3-Year Study Shows How Managers Are Made," *Nation's Business*, vol. 44, no. 3 (March 1956), pp. 90-91.

68. *Professional Management in General Electric Book Three*, p. 89.

69. *Manager Development Study: Basic Report on Manager Development Plan* (New York: Management Consultation Services Division, General Electric Company, July 1953), pp. v-vi.

70. Harris, p. 90.

71. *Manager Development Study*, p. 2.

72. "Chairman of the Board and Chief Executive Officer Position Guide," 4/24/58, *General Electric Organization and Policy Guide*, pp. 6-7.

73. Harris, p. 90.

74. Quoted in Harris, ibid.

75. Joseph M. Guilfoyle, "General Electric U.," *The Wall Street Journal*, vol. 145, no. 104 (May 27, 1955).

76. Interview with William J. Greenwood, Darien, Connecticut, November 29, 1969. Mr. Greenwood was on the same program with Mr. Swope.

77. Guilfoyle, and letter from Lieutenant Colonel L.F. Urwick, June 24, 1969.

78. "GE Institute Near End of Run—Now What?" *Business Week*, March 4, 1961, p. 51.

79. Ibid., p. 50.

80. Interview with Hugh Estes, New York, July 30, 1969. Mr. Estes said that the school shutdown was used to redesign the curriculum to match the new needs of the employees.

81. "Management Training: An Act of Faith," *Dun's Review and Modern Industry*, vol. 92, no. 6 (December 1968), p. 49. Reprinted by special permission from Dun's, Dun & Bradstreet Publication Corp.

82. Quoted in ibid.

83. "GE Institute Nears End of Run," p. 50.

84. Harris, p. 91.

85. Quoted in ibid., p. 93.

86. "Management Training," p. 46.

87. *Measurements Project—Operational Measurements—Key Result Area No. 6:—Employee Attitudes* (Schenectady, N.Y.: Measurements Service, Accounting Services, General Electric Company, January 1958).

88. Willard V. Merrihue and Raymond A. Katzell, "ERI—Yardstick of Employee Relations," *Harvard Business Review*, vol. 33, no. 6 (November-December 1955), pp. 91-99.

89. *Key Result Area No. 6*, p. 63.

90. Ibid., p. 4.

91. Edward L. Munson, *The Management of Men* (New York: Henry Holt and Co., 1921), p. 740.

92. Earl Brooks, "Getting Results Through Others," unpublished mimeograph used in Organizational Behavior and Theory 120, Graduate School of Business and Public Administration, Cornell University, Fall 1964, p. 2.

93. *Key Result Area No. 6*, p. 5.

94. Ibid., p. 7.

95. Ibid., p. 93.

96. Merrihue and Katzell, pp. 94-95.

97. Ibid., p. 95.

98. Ibid., p. 95.

99. Ibid.

100. Interview with Thomas Gilson, Chairman, Department of Management, Marketing, and Industrial Relations, University of Hawaii, Honolulu, Hawaii, December 8, 1969.

101. See Rensis Likert, *New Patterns of Management* (New York: McGraw-Hill Book Company, Inc., 1961), p. 75.

102. *Key Result Area No. 6*, pp. 26-28.

103. Drucker, *The Practice of Management*, p. 385.

104. *Measurements Project, Part I*, p. 29.

105. U.S. Senate, Committee on Judiciary, *Price Fixing and Bid Rigging in the Electrical Manufacturing Industry*, S. Res. 52, Part 27, 87th Cong., 1st Sess., 1961, p. 16509.

106. Lewis, pp. 39-40.

107. *Measurements Project, Part I*, p. 29.

108. Richard Austin Smith, "The Incredible Electrical Conspiracy, Part I," *Fortune*, vol. 63, no. 4 (April 1961), p. 137.

109. Richard Austin Smith, "The Incredible Electrical Conspiracy, Part II," *Fortune*, vol. 63, no. 5 (May 1961). Also see "General Electric and the Price Conspiracy Cases," Northwestern University, School of Business, 1962, Intercol-' legiate Case Clearing House, No. ICH 9 G 146, and Harris.

110. U.S. Senate, Part 28, p. 17723.

111. *General Electric Company Annual Report 1960*, p. 22.

112. *General Electric Company Annual Report 1961*, p. 22, and *General Electric Company Annual Report 1962*, pp. 24-25.

113. Lewis, p. 41.

114. Interview with Harold F. Smiddy, Cincinnati, Ohio, August 25, 1969.

115. *Measurements Project, Part I*, pp. 41-42.

116. *Measurements Project, Part I*, p. 37.

117. Ibid., pp. 37-39.

118. Ibid., p. 39.

119. Interview with John Flowers, Manager of Business Analysis and Cost Accounting Consulting, General Electric Company, New York, August 5, 1969. These figures may not be correct, since in 1947 the firm had four staff vice presidents and six operating vice presidents.

120. Ibid.

121. Ibid.

122. Cordiner, *New Frontiers for Professional Managers*, p. 61.

123. "General Electric Organization and Policy Guide, no. 20.6, 'Investments in Facilities,' " 6/15/69, p. 2. The area of appropriations must meet criteria set out for each section of the organization. For the criteria in level four, the six-page policy guide lists a broad outline for determining the criteria.

124. Interview with Paul E. Mills, Glen Ridge, N.J., August 7, 1969.

125. Mary Parker Follett, "The Process of Control," in *Papers on the Science of Administration*, ed. by Luther Gulick and Lieutenant Colonel Lyndall Urwick (Institute of Public Administration, New York, 1937), p. 161.

Chapter 5
The Environment of Decentralization

1. Interview with Philip D. Reed, retired Chairman of the Board, General Electric Company, New York, New York, August 4, 1970.

2. Ibid.

3. Ibid.

4. Interview with Harold F. Smiddy, retired Vice President, Management Consultation Services, General Electric Company, Cincinnati, Ohio, August 23, 1969.

5. Peter F. Drucker, *Concept of the Corporation* (New York: John Day Company, 1946), p. 75. (Rev. ed. 1972.)

6. Edward M. Currie, "The Importance of Human Relations in Decentralization: A Study of GE," unpublished Master's thesis, Iowa State University, 1965, p. 10.

7. *Manager Development Study, Appendix V, Findings On Quantitative Needs* (Management Consultation Services Division, General Electric Company, April 1953), pp. A-8, A-9.

8. *General Electric Company Annual Report 1962*, p. 33.

9. Ibid.

10. Interview with Jack S. Parker, Vice Chairman of the Board, General Electric Company, New York, New York, July 1, 1970.

11. As I See It: An Interview with Retired General Electric Chairman Ralph Cordiner," *Forbes*, vol. 100, no. 8 (October 15, 1967), p. 31.

12. Interview with Paul E. Mills, retired Manager, Organization Consulting Services, General Electric Company, Glen Ridge, New Jersey, August 7, 1969.

13. Ibid.

14. Interview with Philip D. Reed, New York, August 4, 1970.

15. "Mr. Wilson at Work," *Fortune*, vol. 35, no. 5 (May 1947).

16. Interview with Paul E. Mills, Glen Ridge, New Jersey, August 7, 1969.

17. Interview with Thomas A. Gouger, retired Consultant, Management Consultation Services, General Electric Company, Rye, New York, August 24, 1970.

18. Interview with Paul E. Mills, retired Manager, Management Consultation Services, General Electric Company, Glen Ridge, New Jersey, August 7, 1969.

19. Ibid.

20. Ibid.

21. Ibid.

22. Harold F. Smiddy, "Decentralization—Next Stage?" unpublished notes, New York, October 24, 1951.

23. Interview with Harold F. Smiddy, Cincinnati, Ohio, August 25, 1969.

24. Ibid.

25. Ibid.

26. Ibid.

27. Donald R. Webb, Management Consultation Services, unpublished notes written in 1957, p. 5.

28. Interview with John Flowers, Manager of Business Analysis and Cost Accounting Consulting, General Electric Company, New York, August 5, 1969.

29. Ralph J. Cordiner, *New Frontiers for Professional Managers* (New York: McGraw-Hill Book Company, Inc., 1956), p. 54.

30. Webb, p. 2.

31. Interview with Paul E. Mills, Glen Ridge, New Jersey, August 7, 1969.

32. Ibid.

33. Webb, p. 7.

34. Ibid., p. 8.

35. Ibid.

36. Ibid., p. 8.

37. William J. Greenwood, "Organization Tools," unpublished talk to Advanced Management Course, Crotonville, N.Y., January 30, 1956.

38. *Measurements Project, Part I, The Overall Project* (Schenectady, N.Y.: Budgets and Measurements Services Department, General Electric Company, January 1954).

39. Webb, p. 24.

40. Ibid., p. 25.

41. Ibid.

42. Ibid.

43. Ibid.

44. Alvin A. Butkas, "The GE Puzzle," reprinted by special permission from *Dun's*, July 1970, Copyright, 1970, Dun & Bradstreet Publication Corp.

45. Interview with Philip D. Reed, New York, August 4, 1970.

46. Butkas, p. 38.

47. Interview with Philip D. Reed, New York, August 4, 1970.

48. Butkas, p. 38.

49. Peter F. Drucker, *Technology, Management and Society* (New York: Harper & Row, 1970), p. 144. Philip Reed disputed this statement in an interview August 4, 1970, saying: "If all had gone well we would have had profits by 1963-64."

50. Peter F. Drucker, *The Age of Discontinuity* (New York: Harper & Row, 1969), p. 62.

51. Butkas, p. 36.

52. Ibid., p. 37.

53. Interview with Paul E. Mills, Glen Ridge, New Jersey, August 7, 1969.

54. Frank F. Gilmore, *Formulation and Advocacy of Business Policy* (Ithaca, New York: Cornell University Press, 1968), Chapter 1, pp. 6-34.

55. Henri Fayol, "Administration Theory in the State," *Papers on the Science of Administration*, ed. by Luther Gulick and L. Urwick (New York: Institute of Public Administration, Columbia University, 1937), p. 105.

56. James O. McKinsey, "Adjusting Policies to Meet Changing Conditions," *General Management Series*, no. 116 (New York: American Management Association, 1932).

57. Melvin T. Copeland, "The Job of an Executive," *Harvard Business Review*, vol. 18, no. 4 (Winter 1940), pp. 148-1960.

58. Gilmore, p. 7.

59. Peter F. Drucker, *The Practice of Management* (New York: Harper & Row, 1954). For an in-depth analysis of this closed loop or modern objective setting, see Frank F. Gilmore and Richard G. Brandenburg, "Anatomy of Corporate Planning," *Harvard Business Review*, vol. 40, no. 6 (November-December 1962), pp. 61-69.

60. Interview with Paul E. Mills, Glen Ridge, New Jersey, August 7, 1969.

61. Ibid.

62. Ibid.

63. Ibid.

64. Ibid.

65. Ibid.

66. Ibid.

67. Ibid.

68. Ibid.

69. Letter from Charles E. Wilson, retired President, General Electric Company, April 14, 1970.

**Chapter 6
Evaluation of the Individual
Under Decentralization**

1. Columbia University Graduate School of Business, *Round Tables on Management of Expanding Organizations*, November 1953-March 1954, Minutes of 4th meeting.

2. Ibid., p. 2.

3. Ibid., p. 5.

4. Peter F. Drucker, *Managing for Results* (New York: Harper & Row, 1964), Chapter 4.

5. Peter F. Drucker, *The Practice of Management* (New York: Harper & Row, 1954), p. 131.

6. Ibid., pp. 131-32.

7. Raymond Villers, "Control and Freedom in a Decentralized Company," *Harvard Business Review*, vol. 32, no. 2 (April-May 1954), p. 96.

8. Letter from Lemuel R. Boulware, retired Vice President, General Electric Company, March 10, 1970.

9. Boulware letter.

10. Interview with William J. Greenwood, Darien, Connecticut, November 23, 1969.

11. Business reviews are conducted by the group and division managers over a department, along with the services heads, to evaluate operating departments along the lines laid down by the eight key result areas. They are frequently called with less than a week's notice. See *Business Week*, April 19, 1952, p. 123.

12. Interview with William J. Greenwood, Darien, Connecticut, November 23, 1969.

13. Arthur Vinson, "General Electric's Services Division," *Planning, Managing, and Measuring the Business* (New York: Controllership Foundation, Inc., January 1955), p. 10.

14. Interview with William J. Greenwood, Darien, Connecticut, November 23, 1969.

15. Boulware letter.

16. Lemuel R. Boulware, *The Truth About Boulwarism: Trying To Do Right Voluntarily* (Washington: Bureau of National Affairs, Inc., 1969), especially pp. 92-96.

17. Boulware letter.

18. Ibid.

19. *Measurements Project, Part I, The Overall Project* (Schenectady, N.Y.: Budgets and Measurements Services Department, General Hectric Company, January 1954).

20. Interview with Jack S. Parker, New York, July 1, 1970.

21. Frank Greenwood, *Casebook for Management and Business Policy: A Systems Approach* (Scranton, Pa.: International Textbook Company, 1968), p. 144.

22. Lecture by Ronald B. Shuman, in Principles of Management course, University of Oklahoma, Norman, Oklahoma, April 24, 1967.

23. Ronald B. Shuman, *The Management of Men* (Norman, Oklahoma: University of Oklahoma Press, 1948), pp. 182, 184.

24. Peter F. Drucker, *Landmarks of Tomorrow* (New York: Harper & Row, 1959), pp. 90-91.

25. Peter F. Drucker, *The Age of Discontinuity* (New York: Harper & Row, 1969), p. 288.

26. Peter F. Drucker, *Technology, Management, and Society* (New York: Harper & Row, 1970), p. 37.

27. Norman F. Maier, *Psychology In Industry*, third ed. (Boston: Houghton Mifflin Company, 1965), p. 256.

28. A more detailed explanation can be found in General Electric's *Manager Development Study* booklets, especially *Appendix I*, "Appraisal Plan for Manager Development" (1953) and *Appendix II*, "Manager's Appraisal Guide" (1953).

29. Interview with William J. Greenwood, Darien, Connecticut, November 23, 1969.

30. Interview with Jack S. Parker, New York, July 1, 1970.

31. Ibid.

32. Ibid.

33. Boulware letter.

34. Ibid.

35. Douglas McGregor, "An Uneasy Look at Performance Appraisal,"

Harvard Business Review, vol. 35, no. 3 (May-June 1957), p. 91. Also see McGregor, *The Professional Manager* (New York: McGraw-Hill Book Company, Inc., 1967), Chapter 8, especially p. 131.

36. Donald R. Webb, Management Consultation Services, unpublished notes written in 1957, p. 9.

37. Ibid., p. 10.

38. Interview with Dr. Herbert H. Meyer, Consultant, Behavioral Research Service, General Electric Company, Darien, Connecticut, August 25, 1970.

39. *Professional Management in General Electric Book Three, The Work of a Professional Manager* (New York: General Electric Company, 1954), pp. 59-60.

40. McGregor, "An Uneasy Look . . . ," p. 90.

41. *Professional Management in General Electric Book Three*, p. 73.

42. Robert Townsend, *Up The Organization* (New York: Alfred A. Knopf, 1970), p. 142.

43. *Professional Management in General Electric Book Three*, p. 73.

44. Harry Arthur Hopf, "Business Management and the Scientific Point of View," *The Engineering Journal* (Canada), vol. 20, (December 1937).

45. H.D. Metcalf and L. Urwick, eds., *Dynamic Administration: The Collected Papers of Mary Parker Follett* (New York: Harper & Brothers, 1941), p. 213.

46. Ray E. Brown, *Judgment in Administration* (New York: McGraw-Hill Book Company, Inc., 1966), pp. 65-66.

47. *Professional Management in General Electric Book Four, The Work of a Functional Individual Contributor* (New York: General Electric Company, 1959), pp. 189-90. This is taken from Drucker's *The Practice of Management*, p. 150.

48. Dr. Meyer is a Consultant in Behavioral Research Service, General Electric Company.

49. Herbert H. Meyer, Emanuel Kay, and John R.P. French, Jr., "Split Roles in Performance Appraisal," *Harvard Business Review*, vol. 43, no. 1 (January-February 1965), pp. 123-29.

50. Ibid.

51. E. Kay, J.R.P. French, Jr., and H.H. Meyer, "A Study of the Performance Appraisal Interview," (New York: Management Development and Employee Relations Services, General Electric Company, March 1962), p. 35.

52. Interview with Herbert H. Meyer, Darien, Connecticut, August 25, 1970.

53. Ibid.

54. Meyer, Kay, and French, p. 35.

55. Interview with Herbert H. Meyer, Darien, Connecticut, August 25, 1970.

56. "A Comparison of a Work Planning Program with the Annual Performance Appraisal Interview Approach," (Crotonville, N.Y.: Management Development and Employee Relations Services, General Electric Company), p. 2.

57. Hugh Estes, "The Ethics of Applied Behavioral Science," Speech, Cornell University Conference, New York, April 8, 1964.

58. Ibid.

59. Interview with Dr. Rensis Likert, Director, Institute for Social Research, University of Michigan, Honolulu, Hawaii, March 9, 1970.

60. Rensis Likert, *New Patterns of Management* (New York: McGraw-Hill Book Company, Inc., 1961), Chapter 14.

61. Paul Hersey and Kenneth H. Blanchard, *Management of Organizational Behavior* (Englewood Cliffs, N.J.: Prentice-Hall, 1969), p. 54.

62. Interviews with Harold F. Smiddy, Honolulu, Hawaii, October 1, 1970; Paul E. Mills, Glen Ridge, New Jersey, August 7, 1969; William J. Greenwood, Darien, Connecticut, January 5, 1970; Hugh Estes, Manager, Organization Planning, General Electric Company, New York, July 30, 1969.

63. Interview with William J. Greenwood, Darien, Connecticut, April 10, 1970.

64. Webb, p. 10.

65. These claims are documented from Ibid., and interviews with Paul Mills, Glen Ridge, New Jersey, August 7, 1969; William J. Greenwood, Darien, Connecticut, April 10, 1970; and George Chamberlin, Vice President and Controller, Scott Paper Company, Philadelphia, June 30, 1970, all former employees of the General Electric Company.

Chapter 7
Entrepreneurship Planning and
Decentralization

1. Peter F. Drucker, *Technology, Management and Society* (New York: Harper & Row, 1970), p. 133.

2. Ibid.

3. Interview with Peter F. Drucker, New York, September 29, 1970.

4. Interview with Peter F. Drucker, New York, October 19, 1970.

5. Interview with William J. Greenwood, Darien, Connecticut, November 23, 1969.

6. Interviews with various General Electric employees who wish to remain anonymous.

7. Copyright © 1965 by Stanyan Music Company.

8. See Alvin A. Butkas, "The G.E. Puzzle," *Dun's Review*, vol. 96, no. 1 (July 1970); Allan T. Demaree, "G.E.'s Costly Ventures into the Future," *Fortune*, vol. 82, no. 4 (October 1970); Interview with Peter F. Drucker, Montclair, New Jersey, December 19, 1970. See also Chapter 4 of this book.

9. Interview with Peter F. Drucker, Montclair, New Jersey, November 9, 1970.

10. Alfred Chandler, Jr., *Strategy and Structure: Chapters in the History of the Industrial Enterprise* (Cambridge, Mass.: The M.I.T. Press, 1962), p. 366.

11. Interview with Peter F. Drucker, New York, October 19, 1970.

12. Chandler, p. 383.

13. Ibid.

14. Peter F. Drucker, *The Age of Discontinuity* (New York: Harper & Row, 1969), p. 43.

15. Butkas, Demaree. See also Chapter 5.

16. Interview with John B. McKitterick, Vice President—Corporate Planning, General Electric Company, New York, October 20, 1970.

17. Drucker, *Technology, Management and Society*, p. 109.

18. Ibid., p. 110.

19. Peter F. Drucker, *The New Society* (New York: Harper & Brothers, 1950), p. 208.

20. Ibid.

21. Ray A. Killian, *Managing By Design* (New York: American Management Association, 1968), p. 55.

22. Interviews with Jack S. Parker, Vice Chairman, General Electric Company, New York, July 1, 1970; John B. McKitterick, New York, October 20, 1970; Melvin Weber, Manager, General Electric Company, Bridgeport, Connecticut, September 30, 1970; see also Fred J. Borch, General Announcements, no. 499, General Electric Company, May 25, 1970.

23. Interview with John B. McKitterick, New York, October 20, 1970.

Chapter 8
Conclusion

1. "Lessons of Leadership: Part XXXIV: Inspiring Teamwork," *Nation's Business*, vol. 56, no. 3 (March 1968), p. 42.

2. Chandler, p. 366.

3. General Electric Company, *Organization & Policy Guide*, Tab, "Introduction and Contents," April 8, 1959 (also found in Guides issued July 16, 1954, and April 8, 1961), p. 2.

4. Quoted by Harold F. Smiddy in "The Objectives, Work, Organization and Personnel of Management Consultation Services Division," speech at the Waldorf-Astoria Hotel, New York, January 7, 1954, p. 10.

5. As previously quoted, Paul E. Mills, interview, August 7, 1969, Glen Ridge, New Jersey.

6. Henry C. Metcalf and L. Urwick, *Dynamic Administration, The Collected Papers of Mary Parker Follett* (New York: Harper & Brothers, 1940), p. 146.

Name Index

Subject Index